Jaimini Jyotisha Series

Lakshmana Suri's

Jyotih Pradeepika

English translation & exposition of a
partial but unprecedented manuscript

Dr. K. GURU RAJESH

For copies write to:

Email:
raj91979@gmail.com
rajesh_kotekal@rediffmail.com

PREFACE

After successfully bringing out my English translation of Raghava Bhatta's Jataka Sara Sangraham at the end of 2018, I had taken up the task of translation of Sutrartha Prakashika of Akumalla Nrusimha Suri. While going through the three versions of Lakshmana Suri's Jyotih Pradeepika commentary in my collection, I could see that both Sutrartha Prakashika and Jyotih Pradeepika are almost same in their treatment of the Jaimini Sutras. Hence, I started working on the English translation of both of them with an intention of presenting them in a single book. Midway into the job, I received another manuscript of Jyotih Pradeepika from Sri G.V. Prabhakara Murthy Garu of Bangalore. This version was written down by late Sri Madhura Krishna Murthy Sastry Garu from the manuscript of his Guru Sri Sripada Venkataramana Daivajna Sharma Garu. I could immediately recognize that, except for the opening lines, this Jyotih Pradeepika manuscript is very different from the three versions I have with me. I was awestruck after going through this manuscript and it completely pulled my attention away from my work on Sutrartha Prakashika.

This manuscript is partial and discusses only 24 Sutras of the 1st quarter of chapter 1 of Jaimini Sutras. However, within this brief text, I could glean the intellectual brilliance of the author who treated most of the Sutras in an altogether different way. His unique way of defining the Argalas, Atma Karakas, four kinds of Chakras, Upajeevya Raja Yogas, and various Dasa systems etc. are unprecedented. The highlight of the work is the demonstration of the concepts using many real-life horoscopes. This work also has a great historical value as it demonstrates the Upajeevya Raja Yogas by presenting the horoscopes of Akbar, Shah Jahan, and Aurangzeb.

There appears to be more than one Lakshmana Suri as evident from the different versions of available Jyotih Pradeepika manuscripts. I suspect at least two different persons on the basis of manuscripts I have seen. The author of this present version likely belongs to the southern part of India as he discusses horoscopes of people bearing Tamil and Telugu names like Varadaraja Perumallu besides the horoscope of the famous Appayya Deekshita. The birth years in CE of the eight natives as per the horoscope details are respectively: 1608, 1621, 1606, 1607, 1591, 1542, 1592, and 1618.

The latest among them is horoscope-2 belonging to the year 1621 CE. Thus, we can safely presume that our author might have lived in the 17th century.

This small work, though partial and sketchy because of the gaps in the manuscript, is a treasure-trove of Jaimini Jyotisha. The author offers an entirely different way of interpreting the Nidhyatu Yogas, Argala analysis, and Drik Dasa calculation and its interpretation. Along with these, the unique way of preparation of the Svamsa Chakra, Pada Chakra, Upapada Chakra, and Graha Chakra; their utility in applying the 2nd, 3rd and 4th quarters of the 1st Chapter of the Jaimini Sutras; application of the Svamsa, Pada and Upapada Chakras for Upajeevya Raja Yogas; the Svamsa Chakra Karaka Dasa calculation and interpretation; the Atmano Bhavapamsa Dasa calculation and interpretation; the Bhava Lagna Karaka Dasa calculation and interpretation – all these are worthy of detailed study and research making us realize the depth and grandeur of the Jaimini system.

This is an utter injustice that some scholars of Jaimini Jyotisha discard the valuable commentaries of Raghava Bhatta, Nrusimha Suri, Lakshmana Suri, Parameshvara Yogindra, Nilakantha, Somanatha Mishra, Krishna Mishra etc. by expressing doubt about the caliber and reliability of these learned commentators even without conducting the required diligent study. But, they look for guidance by over-stretching the matter available in the Brihat Parasara Hora Sastra. Nevertheless, an open-minded and sensible student can easily recognize the great practical utility of these commentaries because, unlike conventional Jyotisha classics, some of them demonstrate the concepts by providing real-life example horoscopes which stands as a proof of well-flourishing and successful practice of the Jaimini Jyotisha. Therefore, treading the path shown by yesteryear doyens like Sri Madhura Krishna Murthy Sastry and Sri Iranganti Rangacharya, who painstakingly collected and studied various manuscripts scattered all over India, is the right direction to reinstate the Jaimini system to its original splendor. Inspired by them and with the blessings of Lord Sri Hari and my Gurus, I have embarked on a difficult but highly fulfilling journey of bringing out the available commentaries and expositions of the Jaimini Jyotisha as much as possible so that the discerning Jyotisha enthusiasts will get access to this wealth of knowledge and wisdom.

Ultimately, I hope to come out with a comprehensive and composite method of horoscopic interpretation applying Jaimini methods alone by incorporating the insights gained from various commentaries.

In this book I have presented the Sanskrit text of the manuscript in Devanagari followed by my English translation and detailed notes. I have presented the manuscript in the available form. Wherever I felt a need of some correction I have 'strikethrough' the original text and provided the correct text as per my understanding. At some places I tried to supply the missing text by guessing the words from the adjacent parts of the manuscript. After the manuscript text and its English translation, I have summarized the insights and inferences in a separate section segregating the concepts topic-wise. This would help research minded readers who want to further work on these concepts using actual horoscopes. To the end of the book, the scanned copy of the original manuscript of 19 pages written in Telugu script by Sri Madhura Krishna Murthy Sastry is included for reference. In connection with my work, I should also admit the element of error that might have crept because of the poor understanding at the places where there are gaps in the manuscript text. Nevertheless, I hope the readers would appreciate the hard work that goes in comprehending and presenting a manuscript of this kind dealing with a complex subject like Jaimini system handicapped by the gaps in the manuscript text. I sincerely pray that the full version of this manuscript shall be discovered in near future. The next edition of this book may include full manuscript if we succeed in tracing it out from the manuscript libraries. Otherwise, the next edition will be provided with the insights obtained from extensive study of the concepts proposed in this partial manuscript by incorporating numerous real-life horoscopes.

The dates of the example horoscopes have been checked using the Jagannatha Hora software of Sri P.V.R. Narasimha Rao for which I express my sincere thanks. I have used traditional Lahiri Ayanamsa for the purpose and the debate of correctness or otherwise of various Ayanamsas is immaterial for the present translation work. Interested researchers of Siddhanta division of Jyotisha may further consider working on the details of example horoscopes given by the author.

I am indebted to Sri G.V. Prabhakara Murthy Garu for providing me this manuscript which opened an entirely different world of Jaimini to me. I am grateful to my dear friend Sri Shanmukha for all the help he extended in my Jaimini studies. In preparing the present book also, his inputs have been of huge advantage to me. I will be lacking in my duties if I do not acknowledge with devotion the contribution of late Sri Madhura Krishna Murthy Sastry Garu to the world of Jaimini seekers. He had meticulously copied down this manuscript from his Guru's library in Vilambi Samvatsara in 1958, exactly 60 years ago as we are in the same Vilambi Samvatsara now. My sincere thanks are also due to the readers of my earlier book on Jaimini, Jataka Sara Sangraham, for their support and encouragement. I hope this book would open a new world for Jaimini enthusiasts. I sincerely request research-minded Jaimini students to vigorously test the concepts proposed in this work and come out with their valuable insights.

K. Guru Rajesh
Vilambi Magha Suddha Ekadashi, 2019
Bhubaneshwar

श्रीरस्तु

श्री महागणाधिपतये नमः

जैमिनीयसूत्रव्याख्यानं

वन्दे ~~सूर्य~~....(धामनिधिं) कलानिधिमतिप्रीत्यायुतं मंगलम्
छन्दोगेषुबुधं गुरुं वरकविं सर्वेनमस्यन्ति यम् ।
दैत्यानामशनिं तधागततमोरूपं च केतुं जगत्-
रक्षायै ग्रहरूपमाश्रितमहं वन्दे ~~शुभाकांक्षया~~ (शुभार्थप्रदम्) ॥

I worship the lord who is an abode of effulgence and also an embodiment of all lustre (arts). He is full of compassion and is the personification of all auspiciousness. He is the ultimate master of Samaveda where the Mantras are sung to metre. He is the great preceptor of entire creation and he is the omniscient being worshipped by everyone. He is like a thunderbolt for the evil Daityas and led them to darkness and decay through his form of Buddha. He is known as Dhuma Ketu with his Kalki incarnation. To protect the entire creation he has assumed the forms of the nine planets. I salute such lord who showers auspicious blessings on his devotees.

NOTES: This Shloka written as a prayer to Lord Vishnu incorporates the names of the nine planets in an intelligent way. The word *Dhamanidhi,* which means abode of effulgence, also refers to the Sun. The word *Kalanidhi,* which means embodiment of lustre and arts, also refers to the Moon. The word *Mangala,* which means auspiciousness, also refers to Mars. The word *Budha* referring to Mercury is incorporated in the statement *Chandogeshu Budham.* The words *Guru* meaning teacher and *Kavi* meaning knowledgeable also refer to Jupiter and Venus respectively. The word *Ashani* which means thunderbolt incorporates *Shani*, the name of Saturn. The word *Tamo* in *Tathagata Tamorupam* refers to Rahu while *Ketu*, the name of planet Ketu, is used to refer the *Kalki* incarnation.

जैमिनीयस्य सूत्रस्य लक्ष्मणाख्यस्सुधीमणिः ।
ज्योतिःप्रदीपिकां नाम वृत्तिंकुर्वे यथामति ॥

I, named as Lakshmana, who is endowed with good mental acumen, am going to present an exposition on the Jaimini Sutras as per my understanding and intellect, in this work titled *Jyotih Pradeepika.*

इह खलु वेदपुरुषस्य नयनरूपांगभूत ज्योतिश्शास्त्रतत्वं भगवता भर्गेण पार्वत्यै उपदिष्टं | तया स्कन्दाय | तेन गर्गाय | ततः उपदेश..(प्राप्तव)ता कारुणिकेन जैमिनिना लोकानां तत्वबोधाय रचितेषु ~~ज्योतिश्शास्त्रेषु~~ (ज्योतिश्शास्त्रतत्वेषु) ||

This great science of Jyotisha which represents the eyes of the Veda Purusha was instructed to Parvati by her husband Lord Shiva. Parvati passed this knowledge to her son Lord Skanda (also known as Kumara or Subrahmanya) who in turn bestowed this science to Garga Rishi. Rishi Garga taught this knowledge to his pupil Jaimini, who, because of his compassion, formulated the science in the form of aphorisms to teach the entire world.

NOTES: Here, the hoary Parampara of this divine science is mentioned. As per this text, Jyotisha originated from Lord Shiva as opposed to the other traditions where Lord Brahma is considered as the originator.

उपदेशं व्याख्यास्यामः ||१||

उपदेशं | उः शिवस्य पदे चरणौ उपदे | शंकरतया (शमिति) | शिवपादाब्जस्मरणरूप-मंगलपूर्वकं कृतमिदं (आद्यं) प्रतिज्ञासूत्रम् | उपदिश्यते सकलज्योतिश्शास्त्रमनेनेत्युपदेशः | ज्योतिश्शास्त्रं स्वस्मै गर्गकृतोपदेशोवा | तं व्याख्यास्यामः | प्रकटीकरिष्यामः इत्यर्थः | एतच्छास्त्रे विशिष्योपदेशं संज्ञापरिभाषादिकं विविच्य कथइष्याम.....(इत्यर्थः) |..(अ)त ऊर्ध्वमापादपरिसमाप्तेः क्वचिदन्यत्रापीति वेदितव्यम् |

The word *U* represents lord Shiva and *Pade* indicates his lotus feet. *Sham* stands for auspiciousness. Thus, in this first Sutra *Upadesham*, the Rishi Jaimini remembers the lotus feet of Lord Shiva to pray for happiness and prosperity for the students of this subject. The word *Upadesham* also represents all the secrets of the science taught to Jaimini by his teacher Garga, and *Vyakhyasyamah* says that Jaimini is now going to discuss such great teachings of sage Garga in these aphorisms. This means, in this treatise, the specific principles of the subject along with the technicalities will be expounded and discussed clearly. This meaning applies till the ending of this quarter and also to some of the specific topics of the other chapters.

अभिपश्यन्ति ऋक्षाणि ||२||

ऋक्षाणि राशयः अभिपश्यन्ति | अभिमुखराशिं पश्यन्ति | अत्रेयं प्रक्रिया | चरोराशिरभिमुखं स्थिरं पश्यति | स्थिरोराशिरभिमुखं चरं पश्यति | उभयराशिरभिमुखमुभयमेव पश्यति | तत्र च | ओजश्चेदष्टमं युग्मश्चेत्षष्ठम् | उभयः ओजश्चेच्चतुर्थं युग्मश्चेद्दशममिति विवेकः |

The signs will aspect their opposing signs. This means, a movable sign will aspect its opposing fixed sign. A fixed sign will aspect its opposing movable sign. Similarly, a dual sign will aspect its opposite dual sign. To make the concept clear, among the movable and fixed signs, the odd signs will aspect the opposite 6th signs while the even signs will aspect the opposite 8th signs. The dual signs, if odd, will aspect the 4th signs from them with opposite aspect while the even dual signs will aspect their 10th signs.

NOTES: In this discussion, the Sammukha signs of the dual signs have been clearly mentioned which matches with other works like Jataka Sara Sangraha. For odd dual signs Gemini and Sagittarius, the respective 4th signs Virgo and Pisces are the Abhimukha or Sammukha signs. For even dual signs Virgo and Pisces, their respective 10th signs Gemini and Sagittarius become the Abhimukha or Sammukha signs.

पार्श्वभेच ||३||

अत्र च शब्दात् पश्यन्त्ऋक्षाणीति द्वयमाकृष्यते | ततश्चायमर्थः | राशयः पार्श्वगतं राशिद्वयं पश्यन्ति | अत्र पूर्वसूत्रे अभिशब्दमात्रोक्तावपि अभिमुखंराशिं गमयन्ति | पृथग्योगकरणं अभिमुखदृष्टेरस्ति-विशेष इति गमयितुम् | अत्रेऽयं प्रक्रिया | चरराशिः पञ्चमं लाभं स्थिरं पश्यति | स्थिरस्तृतीयंनवमं चरराशिं पश्यति | उभयस्तु ओजश्चेत्सप्तमं दशमं च पश्यति | युग्मश्चेच्चतुर्थं .....(सप्तमं) च पश्यतीति | अत्रोभयत्राप्यभियुक्त वचनम् |

चरंधनंविनास्थानं स्थिरमन्त्यंविनाचरम् | युग्मं स्वेनविनायुग्मं पश्यतीत्ययमागमः ||

पार्श्वभेच here, the word *Cha* implies the continuation of the meaning of the words **पश्यन्त्ऋक्षाणि**. This means, the signs will aspect the signs placed on their both sides. In the previous Sutra, the word *Abhi* indicates the aspect on opposite signs. The separate mention of signs on both sides in the present Sutra indicates that the aspect on the opposite signs has some speciality. The method of sign aspect as per this Sutra is - a movable sign will aspect the fixed signs placed in the 5th and 11th from it. A fixed sign will aspect the movable signs placed in the 3rd and 9th from it. An odd dual sign will aspect the dual signs placed in the 7th and 10th from it while an even dual sign will aspect the dual signs placed in the 4th and 7th from it. These are the side aspects of the signs. The Vruddha Karika summing up the meaning of both the Sutras is **चरंधनंविना स्थानं स्थिरमन्त्यं विना चरं | युग्मं स्वेनविना युग्मं पश्यतीतययमागमः** || which means, a movable sign will aspect all the fixed signs excepting the one placed in its 2nd. A fixed sign will aspect all the movable signs excepting the one placed in its 12th. A dual sign will aspect all the other dual signs excepting itself.

तन्निष्ठाश्च तद्वत् ||४||

पश्यन्तीत्यनुवर्तते | तन्निष्ठास्तद्गताः ग्रहाः इत्यर्थः | तद्वदिति | तैः आश्रयराशिभिस्तुल्यं पश्यन्ति | तेनतुल्यमिति वतिः ?| चकारोऽवधारणार्थः | तद्गताग्रहाएव प्रागुक्त चरस्थिरोभयन्यायेन पश्यन्ति | न तु राशय इति सूत्रार्थः |

तन्निष्ठाश्च तद्वत्, here also the application of the word **पश्यन्ति** continues. **तन्निष्ठा** means the planets placed in them. Thus, planets will have aspects same as the signs they are placed in. The word *Cha* here indicates that the planets only have such aspects as indicated for the movable, fixed and dual signs. The signs themselves (unoccupied by planets) do not have such aspects.

ननु ग्रहाएव पश्यन्तीत्युक्तम् | अभिपश्यन्ति ग्रहा इत्येवालम् | अयं च योगो नारंभणीयः | सत्यम् | पृथग्योगकरणात् ज्ञायते राशिदृष्टेरपि कुत्रचिदुपयोगोस्तीति | ततश्च सामान्यतोऽत्र निर्देशः | अर्गळा निध्यातुः ||१|१|४|| पश्चाद्रिपुभाग्ययोः ||१|३|४२|| इत्यत्रोभय ग्रहणम् | तथासति | सग्रहत्वे ग्रहदृष्टिमधिकृत्य ग्रहदशासु अर्गळयोगादिकं विचारणीयम् | अग्रहत्वे राशिदृष्टिमधिकृत्य राशिदशासु विचारणीयम् | इति विवेकः |

A question may be asked here. It is said that only planets have aspects but not the signs. Then, it would have been enough by saying **अभिपश्यन्ति ग्रहाः**. There was no need to mention about the signs. Yes, this question is pertinent. The mention of aspects of signs and planets separately indicates that the sign aspects also have their application at some occasions. For the two Sutras **दारभाग्यशूलस्थार्गळा निध्यातुः ||१|१|४|| पश्चाद्रिपुभाग्ययोः ग्रहसाम्ये बन्धः ||१|३|४२||**, the aspects of both signs and planets need to be considered. Hence, when the signs are occupied by planets, the planetary Dasas are to be taken and the Argalas are to be judged by considering the planetary aspects. When the signs are unoccupied, the sign Dasas are to be taken and the Argalas are to be judged by considering the sign aspects.

अत्रच ज्ञापकांतरम् | व्यये सग्रहे ||१|३|२|| इत्यस्मिन्सूत्रे ग्रहदृष्टि इति वच.....(ग्र)हाणामेव दृष्टिस्स्यात्तत्तदृष्टे इत्येवालम् | अतो ज्ञायते राशिदृष्टेरुभ?योगोस्तीति | अन्यथा व्यावृत्यसंभवात् ननु | एकैकं राशि...योराशयः पश्येयुः तत्र सग्रहत्वाग्रहत्वे संभवतः कमधिकृत्य अर्गळयोगादिकं चिन्तनीयम् | तेष्वपि सग्रहेषु ....|

Another Sutra may be discussed here - **व्यये सग्रहे ग्रहदृष्टेवा श्रीमन्तः** ||१|३|२||. In this Sutra also planetary aspects are mentioned…..hence, it can be concluded that planets only have the aspects. Then it implies that the aspect of signs…otherwise there is a chance of exclusion…. When a few aspecting signs are occupied by planets and some other are unoccupied by planets, what should be considered to determine the Argala Yogas and so on? Here also, the signs having planets…….

उत्तरत्र न न्यूना विबलाश्च ||१|१|८|| इति परिभाषावर्तते | तया परिभाषया अग्रहाल्पग्रहयोरज्या?नत्वात् ग्रहणम् | सग्रहाधिकग्रहयोर्ग्रहण... | एवं च ग्रहाश्चेति योगोस्तु | पश्यन्तीत्यनुषंगात् | उभयदृष्टिस्सिद्धाभवतीतिचेन्न | तन्निष्ठा इति वचनस्य ग्रहचक्रादिवशात् कल्पितग्रहाणां ...त्वेतदर्थत्वात् || ननु | तन्निष्ठाश्च ||१|१|४|| इति सूत्रं ब्रूमः | यथास्थानिवदादेशो नव्विधौ ||..........|| इति व्याकरणसूत्रवत् करणम् | स्वाश्रयकार्यस्यापि प्रतिपत्त्यर्थं || त.......तारस्य || त्रिदशत्रिकोणेतिरूपस्य प्रतिपत्त्यर्थत्वात् |

One of the upcoming Sutras says **न न्यूना विबलाश्च** ||१|१|८||. This means, the signs that have no planets or less number of planets are not to be considered. The signs occupied by planets and having more number of planets are to be considered. Hence, if there are planets there is Yoga. Because of the word **पश्यन्ती**, if it is said that both the sign aspect and planetary aspects are implied, it is not correct. As per the saying **तन्निष्ठा**, the planets arranged in the Graha Chakra and so on….this meaning applies there. …(some Vyakarana rules have been discussed here).

एवं च राशिदृष्टिरपि कुत्रचिदनुगृहीताभवति | प्रयोजनंतु गोचरफलादौ दर्शइष्यामः ||.......क्तं || तन्निष्ठाश्चतद्वदिति | एवं च | शुभत्व-पापत्व-तुंगत्व-नीचत्वादिकं ग्रहद्वारास्थितम् |

In this way Rasi aspects will also be applicable at some instances. Their applicability in transit results and so on will be explained later. ….it is said **तन्निष्ठाश्चतद्वत्**…hence, the results of benefic, malefic, exalted, debilitated and so on are dependent on the planets.

NOTES: By the foregoing discussion, though lot of things could not be comprehended because of the gaps in the manuscript, the following conclusions can be drawn. Aspects of signs are predominantly applied only when they are occupied by planets. Aspects of unoccupied signs are applicable only at a few instances including interpretation of transit results. To support these concepts the author has presented different arguments including some of the Jaimini Sutras.

दारभाग्यशूलस्थार्गळा निध्यातुः ॥५॥

.........(निध्या)तुरिति सामान्योक्तेः । द्रष्टुर्ग्रहस्य राशेर्वा दारभाग्यशूलस्थार्गळा भवन्ति । कोर्थः । अस्मिन् शास्त्रे सर्वत्र राशिभाव स ....या ग्रहणम् । तच्चास्मिन्नेवपादे सर्वत्रसवर्णाभावाराशयश्च ॥१।१।३२॥ इत्यत्रसूत्रे वक्ष्यामः ।

Here, the word निध्यातुः means the aspecting planet or sign. From it, the *Dara Bhagya* and *Shoola* positions will become *Argala*. What does this mean? In this Jaimini Sastra, the signs and houses are mentioned always by using the numerical values of the words applying the Katapayadi system. In this very quarter, this concept will be elaborated at the Sutra सर्वत्र सवर्णाभावाराशयश्च ॥१।१।३२॥.

एवं च । दारा अष्टाविंशतिः । भाग्य चतुर्दश । शूल पञ्चत्रिंशत् । भगणशुद्धौ शिष्टासंख्या चत्वारि । द्वौ । एकादश । अतस्तेषु स्थानेषु स्थिताः द्रष्टुरर्गळा अवष्टब्धकरा भवन्तीत्यर्थः । दारेशदृष्ट्या सुखिनः ॥१।३।३८॥ इत्यादिना उच्चत्वशुभत्वादिना च शुभफलप्रदत्वे शुभान्येव प्रबलयंति । रोगेशदृष्ट्या दरिद्राः ॥१।३।७॥ इत्यादिना नीचत्वपापत्वादिना अशुभत्वमेव प्रबलयंतीति यावत् ॥

Hence, the word *Dara* has got a value of 28, *Bhagya* 14 and *Shoola* 35. After deducting the multiples of 12 (the number of signs and bhavas), the remainders will be 4, 2 and 11. Hence, these positions from the aspecting entity will act as *Argalas* or interferers. As per the Sutra दारेशदृष्ट्या सुखिनः ॥१।३।३८॥, if the exalted or benefic nature of the aspecting planet is causing benefic results, the Argala positions will support and enhance the benefic results only. Similarly, as per the Sutra रोगेशदृष्ट्या दरिद्राः ॥१।३।७॥, if the debilitated and malefic nature of the aspecting planets cause malefic results, the Argala positions will enhance the malefic results only.

NOTES: The readers are requested to pay attention to the last part of the paragraph. It is generally thought that the presence of planets in the Argala positions from the aspecting planet (Nidhyatu) will cause benefic results and their presence in the Virodha Argala places will cause malefic results. However, the author says that the benefic and malefic results depend on the nature of the aspecting planet primarily. The Argala will support the primary influence while the Virodha Argalas counter the primary influence. Thus, if the aspecting planet is malefic in nature or debilitated, its aspect will cause malefic results primarily. Hence, the Argalas forming for such planet will support its malefic results. Contrarily, if the aspecting planet is benefic in nature or exalted, its aspect will cause benefic results and the Argalas for such planet will support the same.

Normally the two Sutras referred by the author are interpreted in a different way. The Sutra **दारेशदृष्ट्या सुखिनः** ||१|३|३८|| means, aspect of the 4th lord would make the natives lead comfortable lives. The Sutra **रोगेशदृष्ट्या दरिद्राः** ||१|३|७|| means, aspect of the 8th lord would make the natives suffer penury. The author has used these Sutras to convey the general meaning that the aspect of exalted planets and planets having lordship over benefic houses from the Janma Lagna will cause benefic results. In contrary, the aspect of debilitated planets and planets having lordship over malefic houses from the Janma Lagna, like the 6th, 8th and 12th houses, will cause malefic results.

कामस्थातु भूयसा पापानां ||६||

काम एकपञ्चाशत् | भगणशुद्धौ त्रयाणांशेषात् तृतीयस्थानस्थिता इत्यर्थः | पापा एकादश | तत्रस्थितानामपेक्षया भूयसा | अयमर्थः | एकादशस्थग्रहापेक्षया तृतीयस्थानांबाहुल्ये अर्गळत्वमेव |
The word *Kama* has a value of 51. After expunging the multiples of 12 the remainder is 3. This indicates the 3rd position. The word *Papa* has a value of 11. Hence, in comparison with the planets placed in the 11, greater number is indicated. This means, when the planets placed in the 3rd house are greater in number than those placed in the 11th house, Argala will be formed.

NOTES: Our author interprets this Sutra in an entirely different fashion. Normally, this Argala, also called as Nirabhasa Argala or Kama Argala, is considered to form when three or more malefic planets are placed in the 3rd from the aspecting planet. It is also understood that there is no Virodha Argala to this. However, our author applies the Katapayadi method to the word *Papa* also and says that if more planets (not necessarily malefic planets, any planets will do) are present in the 3rd sign in comparison with the 11th sign from the aspecting planet, then also an Argala will form.

रिःफनीचकामस्था विरोधिनः ||७||

रिःफ. द्वाविंशतिः | नीच षष्टिः | काम एकपञ्चाशत् | भगणशुद्धौ दश-द्वादश-त्रयाणांशेषात् | तत्रस्था ग्रहदृ.........नः विरुद्धार्गळाभवन्ति | तथा च द्रष्टुर्ग्रहस्य शुभाशुभत्वं पूर्ववदुन्नीय

तद्विपरीतफलजनकत्वमेषामू(ह्यं).....श्च द्रष्टारं शुभदं ग्रहं अशुभदं कुर्वन्ति । अशुभदं शुभदं कुर्वन्तीति यावत् ।

The word *Rihpha* has a value of 22, *Neecha* is 60 and *Kama* is 51. After deduction of multiples of 12, the remainders will be 10, 12 and 3 respectively. The planets placed in these signs will form *Virodha* (opposing) *Argala* for the aspecting planet. Thus, after determining the benefic or malefic nature of the aspecting planet by the previous discussion, opposition to such results should be judged by considering the planets placed in these signs. This means, the planets placed in the *Virodha Argala* positions of 10, 12 and 3 signs will reverse the results of the aspecting planet – if the aspecting planet is to give benefic results, they convert it to malefic. If the aspecting planet is to give malefic results, they induce it to give benefic results.

NOTES: It further becomes clear that the original nature of the aspecting planet becomes the primary factor in determining the benefic and malefic results. The planets in Argala signs support the original influence while those in Virodha Argala signs counter it.

नान्यूना विबलाश्च ॥८॥

दारभाग्यशूल....क्रमेण रिःफनीचकामस्था विरोधिनः । एषां दारादिस्था इति परस्परापेक्षया अल्पत्वनीचत्वादिना विबलस्य च योगदत्वं नास्तीत्यर्थादधिकत्वतुङ्गत्वादिना बलवतां च योगदत्वमस्तीत्युक्तम् । कोटीद्वयस्यतुल्यत्वे पश्चाद्रिपुभाग्ययोः ॥१।३।४२॥ इत्यादि सूत्रद्वयेन योगान्तरत्वं.....मितिज्ञेयम् ॥

For the Argala signs of 4, 2 and 11, the signs 10, 12 and 3 will respectively become the Virodha Argala positions. Among them, the signs being week having lower number of planets or debilitated planets etc. cannot exert their influence or Yoga. Contrarily, the signs being powerful being occupied by more number of planets or exalted planets etc. would exert their influence or Yoga. When both an Argala sign and its Virodha sign are equal in strength, following the two Sutras starting with पश्चाद्रिपुभाग्ययोः ॥१।३।४२॥, it is to be understood that another Yoga of different kind…..would be formed.

NOTES: The Sutras referred by the author are पश्चाद्रिपुभाग्ययोः ग्रहसाम्ये बन्धः । कोणयोः रिपुजाययोः कीटयुग्मयोः दाररिःफयोश्च ।. In the extant Jaimini Sutra literature, both these Sutras are generally combined and presented as a single Sutra. Thus, if both the Argala signs and their respective Virodha Argala signs are equal in strength, Bandhana Yogas are formed based on these two sutras. The first Sutra says that if there is equality in the planetary positions in the 2nd and 12th signs there would be incarceration. The next Sutra attributes the same results to the pairs of 5th and 9th signs, 12th and 6th signs, 3rd and 11th signs, and 4th and 10th signs. However, in the present context of Argalas and Virodha Argalas, the pairs of 2nd and 12th, 3rd and 11th, 4th and 10th are involved. Among the other two pairs of 5th and 9th signs, and 6th and 12th signs, the former will be explained subsequently. Nevertheless, there is a major difference in the way the author applies these two Sutras. Normally, these pairs are referred from the Janma Lagna or Atma Karaka or Pada Lagna to interpret the Bandhana Yogas. But, our author applies these Yogas to the aspecting planet (Yogada).

प्राग्वत्त्रिकोणे ||९||

पूर्वोक्तानां षण्णां स्थानानां षष्ठसप्तमाष्टमेष्वित्यर्थः | तथा हि | द्वितीयदशमयोः कोणं षष्ठः | तृतीयलाभयोः कोणं सप्तमः | चतुर्थद्वादशयोः कोणमष्टमः | एषुस्थिताः ग्रहाः प्राग्वद्भवन्ति | तत्संबन्धराशिद्वयावस्थितग्रहवत् शुभाशुभ-प्रबल-तत्तद्विरुद्धबलजनकत्वादिकं कुर्वन्तीत्ययमर्थातिदिश्यते | अयंभावः | .....द्वादशाद्यपेक्षया निषेधः | तथा निषेधमात्रानुरोधीति | एवं सप्तमाष्टमयोरपि द्रष्टव्यं | तद्द्वयोस्समत्वेतु मिश्रार्गळत्वमपि संभवती.......य......|

Along with the earlier mentioned six positions (three Argala and three Viparita Argala positions), the 6th, 7th and 8th houses are also to be considered. This is because the 6th is a trine to the 2nd and 10th signs. The 7th is a trine to the 3rd and 11th signs while the 8th is a trine to the 4th and 12th. The planets placed in these signs (6th, 7th and 8th signs) will have similar impact as that of their trines (2nd & 10th, 3rd & 11th, 4th & 12th). This means, similar to the effect of planets placed in the other related two signs, they can enhance or reduce the benefic or malefic influence of the aspecting plant. The intent here is,……..with reference to the 12th, this forms an obstruction. In the same way, the 7th and 8th houses are also to be judged. When both of them (2nd and 12th signs) are equal in strength as per these factors, there is the possibility of occurrence of *Mishra Argala* (mixed Argala) also.

NOTES: This is an interpretation entirely different from the other commentators. The author asks us to consider the trinal signs of the Argala and Viparita Argala positions. The planets placed in them support each other. For example, when we are looking for the Argala caused by the 2nd sign from the aspecting planet and its Virodha Argala caused by the 12th sign, we need to consider the planets posited in the trines to the 2nd – 6th and 10th signs, and to the 12th – 4th and 8th signs. The signs of a trine having exalted planets or strong planets or more number of planets will gain upper-hand over the other trine. In this context we should not think that 10th sign is one of the Virodha Argala positions or the 4th sign is one of the Argala positions. We are concerned here only with the Argala caused by the 2nd sign and Virodha Argala caused by the 12th sign. Similarly, other positions are to be judged. When both trines are equal in strength we are told that Mishra Argala will be formed. Unfortunately, the way of interpreting the results of this Mishra Argala is missing because of the gap in the manuscript.

There arises a practical problem when we consider the Argala of the 3rd sign in this context. Its Virodha position is the 11th sign which happens to be its trine. Another sign in the trine is the 7th house. As per the Sutra **दारभाग्यशूलस्थार्गळा निध्यातुः** 11th sign forms the Argala while as per the Sutra **कामस्थातु भूयसा पापानां** the 3rd house also forms the Argala. Hence, even when the planets placed in the 11th house are few in number or weaker than the planets in the 3rd house, an Argala is formed and vice versa. The position of planets in the 7th house thus becomes irrelevant as it supports the Argala in any condition. This shows that Argala will form in any case when the 3rd house or 11th house is occupied by planets, except when equal numbers of planets or planets with equal strength are placed in them.

विपरीतं केतोः ||१०||

केतुः एकषष्टिः | द्रष्टुग्रहाक्रान्तराशिमाश्रित्य द्वादशहृतावशेषात् सएवराशिर्गृह्यते | तस्मात्त्रिकोण इत्यनुवर्तते | तदारभ्यपञ्चमनवमयोरेकस्मिन्ग्रहो विपरीतार्गळत्वं भवति | ततश्च द्रष्टुर्ग्रहस्य शुभदत्वे अशुभदत्वं कल्पयति | अशुभदत्वे शुभदत्वं कल्पयतीत्यर्थः |

The word *Ketu* has the numerical value of 61 which gives 1 as remainder after expunging multiples of 12. This refers to the sign occupied by the aspecting planet. The concept of *Trikona* mentioned in the previous Sutra becomes applicable here also and hence it implies the trines of that sign. Therefore, if a planet occupies a trine from the aspecting planet, a Viparita (Virodha) Argala is formed. Because of this, if the aspecting planet is to give benefic results, they will get modified into malefic results. If the aspecting planet is to give malefic results, contrarily, benefic results will get manifested.

NOTES: For this Sutra also, the author provides an entirely different interpretation when compared with other commentators.

त्रिकोण इति एकत्वं विवक्षितम् । उभयत्र ग्रहसद्भावे योगान्तरत्वम् । तस्यानुशा.......॥ कोणयोरिपुजाययोः ॥१।३।४३॥ इत्यादिना द्वयोर्ग्रहवैषम्येतु अयोगत्वमेव । नन्यूना विबलाश्च ॥१।१।८॥ इत्यत्र निध्यातुरत्य........न्यूनग्रहस्य द्रष्टराश्यर्गळयोर्विषयमपिनास्ति । उपरि । तत्र ग्रहसाम्यइत्यनुषंगात् । अत्रसूत्रे नन्यूनाविबलाश्च ॥१।१।८॥ इत्येतदप्यपेक्षितम् । ततश्च वैपरीत्यमाधिक्ये ।

Here, the word **त्रिकोण** indicates only one trine. When there are planets in both the trines, another kind of Yoga is formed. By these Sutras **तस्यानुशा.......॥ कोणयोः रिपुजाययोः कीटयुग्मयोः दाररिःफयोश्च ॥१।३।४३॥**, when there are unequal planets in the two trines, there will not be Yoga (Viparita Argala). By this Sutra **नन्यूना विबलाश्च ॥१।१।८॥** there is no Argala from the aspecting planet for ...planet. Moreover, consequently, there is equal in the number of planets in both the trines. In this Sutra, the rule of **नन्यूना विबलाश्च ॥१।१।८॥** is also to be applied. From this, when a trine has more strength, reverse to the Yoga (absence of Viparita Argala) is understood to be formed.

NOTES: When one of the two trinal signs of the aspecting planet is occupied by planets, then only Viparita Argala is formed. If the two trinal signs have equal number of planets another Yoga as indicated by the Sutra **कोणयोः रिपुजाययोः कीटयुग्मयोः दाररिःफयोश्च ।** is formed which causes bondage to the native. The meaning of the first Sutra **तस्यानुशा.......॥** is obscure because of the gap in the manuscript. It seemingly refers to the Sutra **तस्यानुसरणादमात्यः ।**. However, I could not make out the purport of this Sutra in this context. When the two trinal signs have unequal number of planets, none of the Virodha Argala or Bandhana Yogas will occur.

द्रष्टग्रहाक्रान्तराशिंविना अन्ये एकादशराशयः अर्गळयोगे न संगृहीतास्स्युः ।

Excepting the sign occupied by the aspecting planet, the rest 11 signs are not to be considered for judging the Argala Yogas.

NOTES: The author unequivocally says that the Argala and Virodha Argala analysis is to be applied only to the sign occupied by the aspecting planet. The remaining 11 signs would not come into the picture. Firstly, the planets aspecting the Lagna, Hora Lagna and Ghati Lagna should be noted. Then, based on the maximum number of Lagnas aspected or the strength of the sign occupied by the planet, only one planet is to be chosen for Argala Analysis. This becomes clear when we study the example horoscopes. The application of the Sutra **नन्यूना विबलाश्च** becomes pivotal in the Argala analysis.

EXAMPLE HOROSCOPE-1

अत्रोदाहरणम् | शकाब्दाः १~~३~~५३० | कीलकसंवत्सर भाद्रपदमासं १० तेदी रात्रि घटिकाः २२ || वरदराज पेरुमाळ्ळु जन्मलग्नं कर्कटकम् | रविस्फुटम् | ५|११|१२|| चन्द्रः | (११)..|११|५१|| कुजः |९|२३|५९|| बुधः |४|२५|१२|| गुरुः |~~७~~(०)|२६|५४|| शुक्रः |५|९|३०|| शनिः |९|०|२६|| राहुः |३|२४|३१| आयुः |५०|| कर्कटकादि वैपरीत्येन क(ालग्नं)......वृश्चिकम् || घटिकालग्नं मेषः ||

Here is an example horoscope. The native, named Varadaraja Perumallu, was born in the year Kilaka corresponding to the Saka year 1530, on the 10th day of the month of Bhadrapada, 22 Ghatis after Sunset. The Lagna is Cancer. The planetary longitudes at the time of birth are: Sun - 5.11°.12', Moon – (11).11°.51', Mars - 9.23°.59', Mercury - 4.25°.12', Jupiter – ~~7~~(0).26°.54', Venus - 5.09°.30', Saturn - 9.00°.26', Rahu - 3.24°.31'. Longevity of the native was 50 years. By counting from Cancer in reverse order…..(the Kala/Hora Lagna) is Scorpio. The Ghatika Lagna falls in Mesha.

NOTES: The Telugu word *Tedi* (probably derived from the Sanskrit word *Tithi*) used here is equivalent to the English word date. It appears that the author has referred to the day of birth in terms of the number of days completed in the solar month after the Sun entered into the sign, while retaining the name of the month of the Amanta Masa of the lunar calendar. This would normally match with the degree occupied by the Sun in the respective sign. The birth date of this native falls between 23rd and 24th of September 1608 AD, at about 2.23 AM. This equals to about 52 Ghatis after

Sunrise. The Hindu calendar matched with the given details and it falls in the Keelaka Samvatsara Bhadrapada Masa Shukla Chaturdashi on 23rd and Purnima on 24th. On 23rd, the Sun was in the 12th degree of Virgo but the Moon is in Aquarius. As we can see further, the Moon cannot be in Aquarius but should be in Pisces which happens only on September 24th. The position of Jupiter is wrongly given in Scorpio instead of Aries, which also matches with the discussion given in the analysis in the subsequent lines.

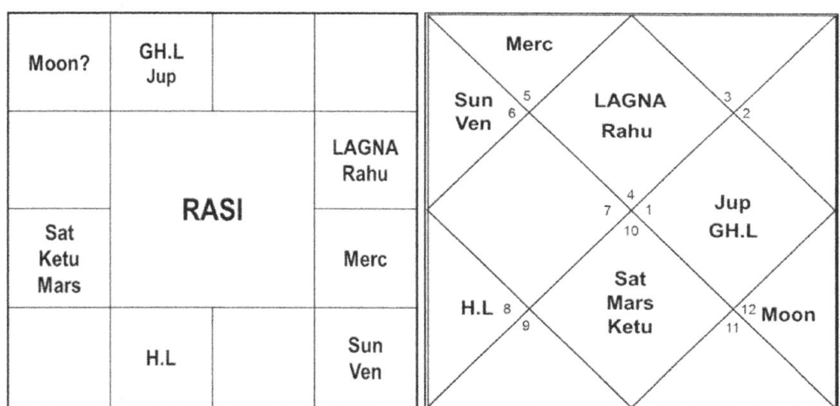

In the process of calculating the Hora Lagna the author considers the fixed duration of 2½ Ghatis as a Hora. This becomes evident when we look into the first three example horoscopes. The other opinion followed by treatises like Jataka Sara Sangraha etc. is to divide the diurnal or nocturnal duration, based on the birth during day or night, into 12 equal parts and considering each part as a Hora. Next, based on the odd and even nature of the Janma Lagna the counting is to be done in zodiacal or reverse order from the Lagna considering one sign for one Hora. The sign thus arrived for the time of birth will be the Hora Lagna. In the present example horoscope, the native was born at around 52 Ghatis after Sunrise. As the Janma Lagna is Cancer, an even sign, the counting is to be done in anti-zodiacal order. Thus counting from the Lagna considering 2½ Ghatis for each sign, the sign arrived for the 52 Ghatis is Scorpio. Therefore, Scorpio is the Hora Lagna.

The process of determining Ghati Lagna (or Ghatika Lagna) seems to be different from other treatises in one aspect. Normally, irrespective of the odd and even nature of the Janma Lagna, Ghati Lagna is determined by counting one sign for one Ghati in zodiacal order up to the time of native's birth. In the present horoscope, as the native was born at about 52 Ghatis after Sunrise, the Ghati Lagna should fall in Libra when counted from the Janma Lagna Cancer in zodiacal order. However, the manuscript says that the Ghati Lagna is in Aries which is only possible if the reckoning from the Janma Lagna is done in anti-zodiacal order. The only possible reason I could attribute to this is the presence of Rahu in the Lagna.

तत्र वृश्चिकस्य दृष्टिराशित्रयसंभवेऽपि । नन्यूना विबलाश्च ॥१।१।९॥ इति अर्गळत्वं मकरस्यैव । ततश्चैकादशे वृश्चिके ग्रहाभावा......गतस्य चन्द्रस्य चतुर्थगतस्यगुरोः सप्तमगस्य राहोः । मकरसहकारित्वेन मकरे उच्चस्वक्षेत्रग्रहसद्भावात् कुजस्य तद्गत .....पञ्चमनवमाधिपतित्वाच्च राजयोगकारिणी बलीयसी मकरदृष्टिः ।

Though the three signs - Aries, Cancer and Capricorn - aspect the Hora Lagna Scorpio, the Argala Yogas will form for Capricorn only as per the rule **नन्यूना विबलाश्च** ॥१।१।९॥. From Capricorn, the 11th sign Scorpio has no planets……Moon, Jupiter placed in the 4th and Rahu placed in the 7th in Cancer (in a trine to Scorpio) will support the benefic aspect of Capricorn. Further, as planets in exaltation and own sign occupy Capricorn……being 5th and 9th lords, the aspect of Capricorn in strength (over Hora Lagna Scorpio) will cause Raja Yoga.

NOTES: No planet aspects the Lagna in Cancer. In the case of Hora Lagna in Scorpio, all the three signs – Capricorn, Aries and Cancer – aspect it as they are occupied by planets. Among them aspect of Capricorn is to be considered alone for Argala analysis as per the rule **नन्यूना विबलाश्च.** Now, coming to the Argala analysis from Capricorn, the 2nd house and its trines are not occupied by any planets. Next, there are no planets in the 11th sign Scorpio while the 3rd and the 7th are occupied by the Moon and Rahu respectively. The Moon forms an Argala as per the Sutra **कामस्था तु भूयसा पापानां**, which is supported by Rahu from a trine as per the rule **प्राग्वत् त्रिकोणे.** Added to this, the position of Jupiter in the 4th from Capricorn also forms an Argala. Mars and Saturn who occupy the aspecting sign Scorpio are in exaltation and own sign respectively thereby causing a strong benefic Yoga. Further, Mars and Jupiter who aspect Scorpio are the

5th and 9th lords respectively from the Janma Lagna thereby forming a Raja Yoga.

मेषस्य तु बुधमात्रदृष्टत्वात् तस्यैवार्गळदत्व..........स्य द्वितीये कन्यायां व्ययापेक्षया ग्रहाधिक्यात् शुभदत्वमेव । तत्पञ्चमे मकरे बहुग्रहसंभवात् । द(शमे).........(वृष)भे ग्रहशून्यतया बुधापेक्षया षष्ठस्य मकरस्य प्राग्वत्त्रिकोणे ॥१।१।९॥ इति कन्यात्वाविशेषात्? शुभसहकारित्वमेव । कन्यायास्स्व.......प्रति भाग्यत्वात् तत्पतिर्बुध इति तद्दृष्टिर्भाग्यकारिणी ।

In the case of Ghatika Lagna in Aries, as it is aspected by Mercury alone, the Argalas are to be judged for Leo only....In the 2nd sign Virgo, there are more planets than the 12th sign Cancer which supports the benefic aspect. This is further strengthened by the placement of many planets in Capricorn, the 5th sign from Virgo (the Argala sign 2nd from the aspecting planet Mercury). There are no planets in (Taurus in the 10th) from Mercury, but the 6th sign Capricorn supports Virgo as per the rule **प्राग्वत्त्रिकोणे** ॥१।१।९॥, this will only enhance the benefic results. ....of Virgo.....being the opposite sign to the 9th? (*Prati Bhagyatva*), the aspect of Mercury on the Ghatika Lagna will cause benefic results only.

NOTES: Next, the Argala analysis for the planet that aspects the Ghatika Lagna in Aries is taken up. Here, the author says that only Mercury from Leo aspects the Ghatika Lagna in Aries. This rules out the position of the Moon in Aquarius as explained at the description of the birth details. Now, the Argala analysis for Leo is to be taken up. The 2nd sign from Leo, Virgo has more planets (two planets Sun and Venus) while the 12th sign Cancer has less planets (only one planet, Rahu). Hence, the Argala will not be destroyed. Further, as per the rule **प्राग्वत्त्रिकोणे** when the trines of the 2nd house Virgo and 12th house Cancer are considered, here also Capricorn, a trine to Virgo, has three planets (Mars, Saturn and Ketu) while Pisces, a trine to Cancer, has only one planet (Moon). Thus, the Argala is strengthened by these dispositions. The last lines of the paragraph are not clear because of the missing words. Virgo is said to have attained a quality of *Prati Bhagyatva* meaning opposite sign to the 9th house that rules *Bhagya* or fortune. Hence, the aspect of Mercury on the Ghatika Lagna is said to be fortunate. Even if the words are considered to be *Pati Bhagyatva*, the text attributes the benefic effect of the 9th house to Virgo and its lord Mercury. To me, it appears - as the 7th house Capricorn is stronger than the Lagna

Cancer by being occupied by strong and more planets, it is considered as the Lagna where by Mercury becomes the 9th lord. This assumption is further strengthened by the fact that the Drik Dasa for this Chakra is taken from the sign Virgo, the 9th from Capricorn.

एवं च । मकरदृष्ट्या राजयोगः । सिंहदृष्ट्या भाग्ययोग इति राजद्वाराभाग्यमितिसिद्धं ॥ का........(दृ)ष्टि फलकत्वात् दृग्दशा ज्ञेयः । तथा हि । कन्यादि प्रथमः खण्डः ए् २६ । मकरादि द्वितीयखण्डः । तत्रापि द्धि(त्रि)चत्वारिंशदुपरि मेषदशा । चतुर्वर्ष.........बहुभाग्ययोगः । आहत्यसप्तचत्वारिंशत् । तदुपरि वृषभदशा पञ्चवर्षा । आहत्य द्विपञ्चाशत् । मकरादि पश्चाद्ग्रहपर्यन्तं ए्? ९ । कुंभ......त्वाद्राह्वन्तं मीनस्य ..॥

Hence, the aspect of Capricorn on Hora Lagna will cause the Raja Yoga while the aspect of Leo on Ghatika Lagna Aries will cause the Yoga for good fortune (*Bhagya Yoga*) which implies that the native will derive good fortune through the rulers. To know the results of the aspects *Drik Dasa* is to be considered. The first portion starting from Virgo has duration of 26 years. The second portion of Drik Dasa starts from Capricorn. In this portion, the Dasa of Aries will commence after 43 years of the native. The four years…(of Aries Dasa)…will bestow the native with superior fortune. The cumulative age of the native up to this point would be 47 years. After that, the Dasa of Taurus will be of 5 years duration. The total would be 52 years. Starting from Capricorn and counting up to the planet placed behind, the duration would be 9 years. For Aquarius….counted up to Rahu….for Pisces….

NOTES: The aspect of 5th lord causes Raja Yoga while the aspect of 9th lord causes Bhagya Yoga. Hence, the aspect of the 5th lord Mars and 9th lord Jupiter on the Hora Lagna in Scorpio is said to cause Raja Yoga while the aspect of Mercury, the 9th lord from the 7th house Capricorn, is said to cause only Bhagya Yoga.

Further, for the analysis of this kind of Raja and Bhagya Yogas, only aspects of the planets are considered and not their placement, strictly following the Sutra **निध्यातुः**.We can see that though benefic and 9th lord Jupiter is placed in Aries in the Ghatika Lagna, our author has considered the aspect of Mercury only for the Yoga analysis.

The Drik Dasa starts from Virgo, the 9th house from Capricorn. The entire Drik Dasa of the 12 signs is divided into three portions of four signs each as per the Sutra **कुजादि त्रिकूट पदक्रमेण दृग्दशा.** Here, the expression *Trikoota Pada Krama* seems to have been interpreted in this way of dividing the Dasa into three groups having four signs each. The first portion of Drik Dasa comprises of the four signs from Virgo to Sagittarius. As the nodes are placed in the Lagna Cancer and the 7th house Capricorn, the Dasa years are to be counted in zodiacal order for the even signs and anti-zodiacal order for the odd signs (Vikruti Chakra, see my English translation of Jataka Sara Sangraha for four kinds of Chakras – Prakruti, Vikruti, Udaya and Graha Chakras). Hence, the durations of the Dasas are: Virgo – 12 years, Libra – 2 years, Scorpio – 3 years, and Sagittarius – 9 years. This totals to a period of 26 years. The next portion of the Drik Dasa comprises of the four signs from Capricorn to Aries. The duration of the Capricorn Dasa is of 9 years. As Capricorn is occupied by its lord Saturn, the Dasa years are to be counted from the Dasa sign Capricorn to the sign occupied by a planet immediately placed behind, as per zodiacal or reverse counting following the Dasa rules. This concept becomes clear by studying the example horoscope given at page 49 where the author says **ग्रहे स्वराशौसति ओजयुग्मन्यायेन पश्चाद्ग्रहांतसंख्यया वर्षानयनं.** Here, among the signs behind Capricorn, Virgo is the first sign occupied by planets -the Sun and Venus. Hence, counting from Capricorn to Virgo following the zodiacal order will give 9 years as the Dasa duration. For calculating the duration of Aquarius Dasa, Rahu is considered as its lord and the counting is done in zodiacal order thereby assigning 6 years to the Dasa. Normally, as per the Dasa rules, reverse order counting is to be done for an odd sign like Aquarius. The logic applied here is unfortunately missing because of the gaps in the manuscript. The next Dasa of Pisces is of 2 years when counted zodiacally up to its lord Jupiter. Thus, the cumulative age of the native by the end of Pisces Dasa would be 43 years (26 + 9 + 6 + 2 years). The next and last Dasa of this portion belongs to Aries which is of 4 years duration when counted in reverse order up to its lord Mars. These four years would give great fortune to the native as Aries is the Ghatika Lagna aspected by Mercury, the 9th lord from Capricorn, having strong Argala in his 2nd sign. By the end of Aries Dasa, the native will complete his 47 years of age. The next Dasa of

Taurus is of 5 years duration when counted in zodiacal order up to its lord Venus. This will cover up to the 52nd year of the native. The native seems to have lived up to his 50th year as given in the description of birth details.

EXAMPLE HOROSCOPE-2

उदाहरणम् | शकाब्दाः १५४२ रौद्रिसंवत्सर पंगुनी(फल्गुन)मासं २४ तेदी बुधदिने उदयादि घटिकाः ६ || ...यपिळ्ळ जननम् | लग्नं १|६|२०|| तत्र स्फुटग्रहाः | रविः |११|२२|५३|| चन्द्रः |२|२८|५२|| कुजः |७|१|३७|| बुधः |०|१६|०|| गुरुः |१|..|..|| शुक्रः |१०|२३|२०|| शनिः |२|१०|३८|| राहुः |७|२२||४९|| काललग्नं मीनम् | घटिकालग्नं वृश्चिकम् |

Another example will be discussed now. This native named …ya Pilla, was born in the year Raudri corresponding to the Saka year 1542, on the 24th day of the month of Phalguna, on Wednesday, 6 Ghatis after Sunrise. The longitudes of the Lagna and nine planets at the time of the native's birth are: Lagna - 1.06°.20', Sun - 11.22°.53', Moon - 2.28°.52', Mars - 7.01°.37', Mercury - 0.16°.00', Jupiter – 1..°..', Venus - 10.23°.20', Saturn - 2.10°.38', Rahu - 7.22°.49'. The Kala Lagna (Hora Lagna) is Pisces while the Ghatika Lagna is Scorpio.

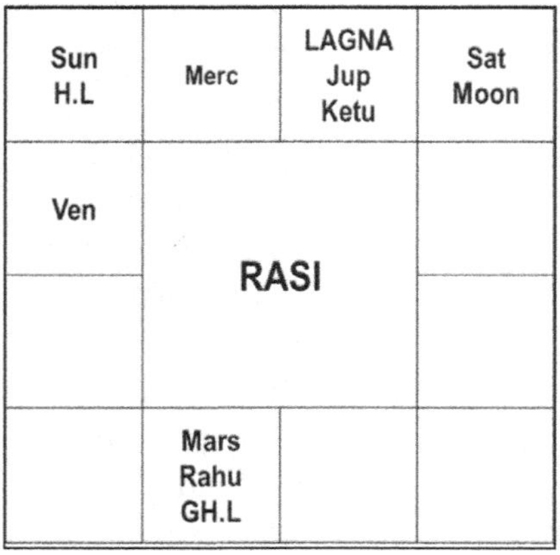

Sun H.L	Merc	LAGNA Jup Ketu	Sat Moon
Ven	RASI		
	Mars Rahu GH.L		

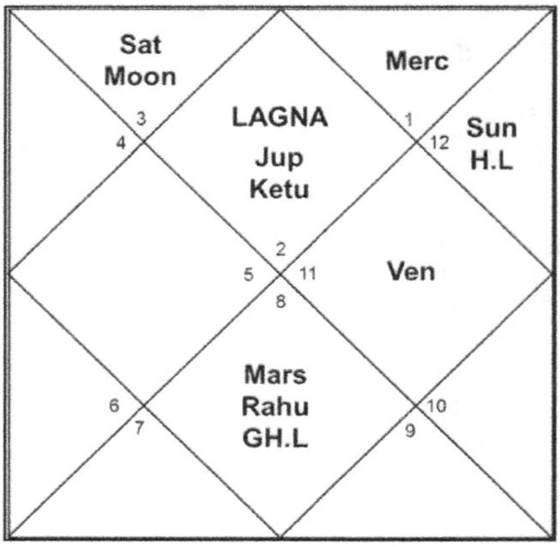

Sat Moon
Merc
3
4
LAGNA
Jup
Ketu
1
12
Sun
H.L
2
5
11
8
Ven
Mars
Rahu
GH.L
6
7
10
9

NOTES: As per the details given, the birth date of the native falls between 31st March and 1st April of 1621 AD, at about 8.30 AM. The position of the Moon would match when 31st March is considered while the position of the Sun will match when 1st April is considered. However, 31st March happens to be a Wednesday matching with the description given by our author. There is a discrepancy in terms of the Hindu calendar here. The planetary dispositions that match with the above dates happen to fall in Durmati Samvatsara Chaitra Shukla Ashtami corresponding to 31st March 1621 AD. The year has changed from Raudri to Durmati, its next year, and the month from Phalguna to Chaitra, the next month. If we have to consider the details given by our author, i.e. Phalguna Masa of Roudri, the date will be around 2nd March 1621. However, the positions of the Sun, Mercury, Venus, Mars and Jupiter do not match with those given in the description if we consider this date.

अत्र श्रीः पत्नीः लाभयोर्दृष्ट्या निराभासार्गळया ॥१।३।२२॥ सप्तमस्य घटिकाभूतस्य वृश्चिकस्य धनपञ्चमाधिपतिना बुधेन दृष्टत्वात् कालस्य भाग्याधिपतिचन्द्राभ्यां दृष्टत्वाज्जातः पुरुषः राजसमो भवति।

Here, following the Sutra **श्रीः पत्नीः लाभयोर्दृष्ट्या निराभासार्गळया ॥१।३।२२॥**, as the 7th sign Scorpio, which also happens to be the Ghatika Lagna is aspected by the 2nd and 5th lord Mercury while the Hora Lagna Pisces is aspected by the 9th lord Saturn along with the Moon, the native will become an equal to a ruler.

NOTES: Among the three – the Lagna, Hora Lagna, and Ghatika Lagna – no planet aspects the Lagna. Hence, aspect on the other two Lagnas is to be considered for Argala analysis. The equivalent of the Sutra **श्रीः पत्नीः लाभयोर्दृष्ट्या निराभासार्गळया** in the extant literature is **पत्नीः लाभयोर्दिष्ट्या निराभासार्गळया**. Here, *Patni* has a numerical value of 1 referring to the Lagna while the word *Labha* refers to the 7th house. Following our author, if the Lagna or the 7th house is aspected by a planet that has un-countered Argalas, the native will be blessed with *Sri* which means wealth and prosperity. Here, the 7th house Scorpio, which is also the Ghatika Lagna, is aspected by the 5th lord Mercury. Further, the Hora Lagna in Pisces is aspected by the 9th lord Saturn and the Moon from Gemini. Note that the Moon happens to be the 9th lord from Scorpio, the 7th house and Ghatika Lagna. Thus, the native will become an equal to a king. The reason for this is explained next.

जन्मकालघटिकास्वेकदृष्टासु राजानः ॥१।३।२४॥ इति त्रयाणां एक ग्रहदृष्ट्या राजत्वम् । द्वयोस्समत्वमित्यभियुक्तवचनात् । तदुक्तं । विलग्नघटिकालग्नहोरालग्नानिपश्यति । एकग्रहोराजयोगो लग्नद्वयमथापिवा। इति।

As per the Sutra जन्मकालघटिकास्वेकदृष्टासु राजानः ॥१।३।२४॥, when all the three among the Lagna, Hora Lagna and Ghatika Lagna are aspected by a planet, the native will become a king. When two of them are aspected by a planet, the native will not be a king but holds a position equal to a king as per the Vruddha Karika विलग्नघटिकालग्नहोरालग्नानिपश्यति। एकग्रहोराजयोगो लग्नद्वयमथापिवा।.

NOTES: In general, this Sutra is interpreted to mean that a single planet is required to aspect the three Lagnas – Janma Lagna, Hora Lagna and Ghatika Lagna. However, our author seems to consider the aspect of different planets on different Lagnas as factors of Raja Yoga. In the present horoscope, the Ghatika Lagna is aspected by Mercury while the Hora Lagna is aspected by the Moon and Saturn. Thus, two of the three Lagnas have planetary aspects on them. Hence, it is said that the native will become an equal to a king.

अत्रार्गळाविचारः । व्ययाद्धने ग्रहाधिक्यात् । लाभेतृतीयेग्रह.....ढस्य राज्यादिविषये उक्तार्गळयोगद्वयं सहकारि।

Now, the Argala Yogas from Mercury are analysed. In comparison with the 12th, the 2nd house has more planets forming an Argala. The planets in the 11th and 3rd...regarding the matters concerned with kingdom etc. the said two Argalas are supportive.

NOTES: In this chart, Mercury aspects Scorpio, the 7th house and also the Ghatika Lagna while Saturn and Moon aspect the Hora Lagna. Thus, following the Sutra नन्यूना विबलाश्च, the Argala analysis is considered for Mercury as he aspects more factors than Saturn and Moon.

When the Argala positions from Mercury are considered, the 2nd from Mercury, Taurus, is occupied by two planets (Jupiter and Ketu) while the 12th sign Pisces has only one planet (the Sun). The 11th house from Mercury has a benefic Venus while the 3rd house Gemini has two malefic planets Saturn and the Moon. As per the Sutra कामस्थातु भूयसा पापानां, the 3rd sign having more number of planets than the 11th will also form an Argala Yoga. In case of the first Argala from the 2nd sign Taurus, though the 8th sign Scorpio which happens to be a trine to the 12th sign Pisces has two planets Mars and Rahu while the trines from the 2nd sign Taurus are empty, this does not cause blemish to the Argala. This is because Scorpio happens to be the Ghatika Lagna occupied by Rahu in exaltation and Mars in own sign. Thus, in matters related to Raja Yoga, these two Argalas support the aspect of Mercury.

कालज्ञानं तु | मेषस्य योगदत्वात्तद्दशायां राजयोगप्राबल्यम् | . . . . . . बुधयुक्त मेषदृष्टशुक्रदशायां च भवति |

The timing of materialization of the Raja Yoga would be during the Dasa of Aries which happens to be the Yogada sign…..it also happens during the Dasa of Venus who is aspected by the sign Aries which is occupied by Mercury.

NOTES: Here, first a sign Dasa like Drik Dasa is considered while the reference to Venus Dasa indicates that a planetary Dasa is being mentioned in the last sentence of the text. This planetary Dasa could be Svamsa Chakra Karaka Dasa or Bhava Lagna Karaka Dasa which will be dealt subsequently.

दृष्टिफलत्वाद्राज्यस्य नवमाधिपदृग्दशानेया | तथाहि |..........| मकरदशा षड्वर्षा ६ | कुंभदशा नववर्षा | आहत्य पञ्चदश | मीनदशा त्रिवर्षा ३ | आहत्य अष्टादश | तदूर्ध्वं मेषदशा षड्वर्षा | अत्र बुधयोगात्प्राबल्यं | आहत्य चतुर्विंशति | २४ | ततः परं वृषभदशा दशवर्षा | तत्रभाग्यकारकग्रहद्वयसंबन्धादत्युच्छ्रयः | ततः मिथुनदशा त्रिवर्षा ३ |

Because the Raja Yoga is formed by the planetary aspects, the Drik Dasa of the 9th lord (9th house?) is to be applied. ….the duration of the 9th sign Capricorn is 6 years. Aquarius Dasa duration is 9 years. The total is 15 years. Next, the Dasa of Pisces would be for 3 years. Total 18 years. Later, the Dasa of Aries will be of 6 years duration. As Mercury occupies Aries, the native will come to prominence. The cumulative years by the end of Aries Dasa would be 24. The next Dasa of Taurus would be for 10 years. As Taurus has the association of two planets that are endowed with the power to cause fortune, the native will experience supreme prosperity and development. Later, the Dasa of Gemini having duration of 3 years will follow.

NOTES: The Drik Dasa is taken from Capricorn, the 9th house from the Lagna Taurus, because, the Lagna Taurus and 7th sign Scorpio appear to be equal in strength. In this case also, as the Lagna is occupied by a node, the Dasa years are counted in zodiacal order for even signs and anti-zodiacal order for odd signs. The Dasa of Capricorn will then be of 6 years when counted up to its lord Saturn in zodiacal order. The next Dasa of Aquarius will be of 9 years when counted up to its lord Saturn in anti-zodiacal order. The cumulative age of the native will be 15 years by the end of Aquarius Dasa. The next Dasa of Pisces will be of 3 years when counted up to its lord Jupiter in zodiacal order. The total will then be 18 years. The next Dasa of Aries would have 6 years duration when counted up to its lord Mars in reverse order. As discussed earlier, the Aries Dasa will bestow Raja Yoga on the native. Thus, the native will complete 24 years of age by the end of Aries Dasa. The next Dasa of Taurus will be of 10 years when counted up to its lord Venus in zodiacal order. It is said that the native will experience greatest prosperity in this Dasa as there is an association of two planets that are empowered to give fortune. I feel that the placement of the Moon and Saturn in the 2nd house is referred here as Saturn is the 9th lord from the Lagna while the Moon is the 9th lord from the 7th house. The next Dasa of Gemini will be of 3 years when counted up to its lord Mercury in anti-zodiacal order.

ततः कर्कटदशा द्वादशवर्षा ||१२|| तत्र प्रथमखण्डवत्सराः ३ | कर्कटकाधिपतेश्चन्द्रस्य मिथुनगतत्वेन तन्नवमादिखण्डकल्पनया ततश्च शुक्रयोगादुच्चत्वं | बुधदृष्टेः राजयोगप्रदत्वंचेति महोन्नति कालः | चत्वारिंशद्वर्षाणि | ततोमीनखण्डस्त्रिवर्षः | अत्र क्रूरयोगात् गुरोश्च क्रूरयोगात् क्लेशकालः |

Following the Dasa of Gemini, the Cancer Dasa will run for 12 years. The duration of first quarter of this Dasa will be for 3 years. As the Moon, the lord of Cancer, is placed in Gemini, the four quarters should be determined starting from the 9th house of Gemini, i.e. Aquarius. As Aquarius is occupied by Venus, the exaltation sign lord of the Dasa lord Moon, the Moon gets the exaltation status. Furthermore, the aspect of Raja Yoga Karaka Mercury on Aquarius indicates a time of greater fortune and status for the native during the first quarter. By the end of the first quarter, the native would have completed his 40th year. Next, the 3 years duration of the second quarter belonging to the next sign Pisces will start. As Pisces is occupied by a malefic planet (the Sun), and also, as its lord Jupiter joins another malefic planet (Ketu), this period will cause difficulties to the native.

NOTES: In this case and also the next example horoscope, the author takes the Dasa of the sign that happens to be the 9th house from any of the three Lagnas for detailed Khanda (quarter) analysis. The total duration of the sign Dasa will be divided into 4 parts. The first part will be assigned to the 9th sign from the sign occupied by the lord of the main Dasa sign. The 2nd, 3rd and 4th parts will be assigned continuously to the 10th, 11th and 12th signs sequentially. In the present case, the Cancer Dasa is considered for Khanda analysis as it is the 9th house from the Ghatika Lagna and 7th house Scorpio. The duration of Cancer Dasa is 12 years when counted up to its lord Moon in zodiacal order. The Dasa duration is divided into four parts each getting a period of 3 years. As the lord of the Dasa sign Cancer, the Moon, is placed in Gemini, the first quarter is assigned to the 9th sign from Gemini – Aquarius. Venus, the lord of exaltation sign of the Dasa lord Moon, is placed in Aquarius thereby causing exaltation for the Moon. Furthermore, it is aspected by the Raja Yoga Karaka Mercury from Aries. Hence, this period of 3 years will prove to be highly beneficial for the native in terms of Raja Yoga. By the end of this quarter the native would have completed 40 years of age (by the end of Aries Dasa he had completed 24 years. Taurus Dasa was for 10 years and Gemini Dasa was for 3 years by the end of which he would have completed 37 years of age. Next, by the end of first quarter of Cancer Dasa represented by Aquarius of 3 years duration, the native would have completed 40 years). The next quarter of 3 years in the Cancer Dasa belongs to the next sign Pisces. As Pisces is occupied by a malefic planet Sun and its lord Jupiter also joins another malefic planet Ketu, the native experiences difficulties in this quarter.

EXAMPLE HOROSCOPE-3

उदाहरणांतरम् | अतःपरमुदाहरणम् | शकाब्दाः १५४२८ ......(पराभवसंव)त्सरं भाद्रपदमासः २५ तेदी उदयादि जन्मघटिकाः ४७ | अ(प्प)य्य दीक्षिताचार्य जननम् | लग्नं |३|७|२|| अत्र स्फुटग्रहाः | रविः |५|२५..|| चन्द्रः |..(७)|२५|२४|| कुजः |८|२५|२६|९|| बुधः |.(५).|..|..|| गुरुः | १०|५|२९|| शुक्रः |४|२१|२९|| शनिः |८|९|३९|| राहुः |५|२|४८|| केतुः |११|२|४८|| आयुः ६०| काललग्नं (मकरः)|| घटिकालग्नं वृषभः ||

Another example Chakra will be discussed now. The native named Appayya Dikshitacharya was born in the year (Parabhava)...corresponding to the Saka year 1528, on the 25th day of Bhadrapada month, 47 Ghatis after Sunrise. The longitudes of the Lagna and the nine planets at the time of birth are: Lagna - 3.07°.02', Sun - 5.25°...', Moon - .(7).25°.24', Mars - 8.25°.26', Mercury - .(5)....°...', Jupiter - 10.05°.21', Venus - 4.21°.29', Saturn - 8.09°.31', Rahu - 5.02°.48', Ketu - 11.02°.48'. Longevity of the native was 60 years. Hora Lagna is...(Capricorn)...Ghatika Lagna is Taurus.

NOTES: As per the details given here, the native was born on 6th October 1606 AD at about 11.50 PM when the Sun's position is considered in the 25th degree of Virgo. The details of the Hindu calendar are – Parabhava Samvatsara, Ashviyuja Shukla Shashti. However, the author says that the month was Bhadrapada instead of Ashviyuja. If Bhadrapada is considered, positions of the Sun and Venus will change – the Sun would be in Leo while the Venus would be in Cancer. Then the date of birth would be between 7th and 10th of September 1606 to match the degrees of the Sun and Moon. Readers may note that the horoscope of Appayya Deekshita has been discussed in a Jaimini work named Vanchinatheeyam also where the planetary position mostly matches with the Bhadrapada Masa description (the Sun in Leo and Venus in Cancer).

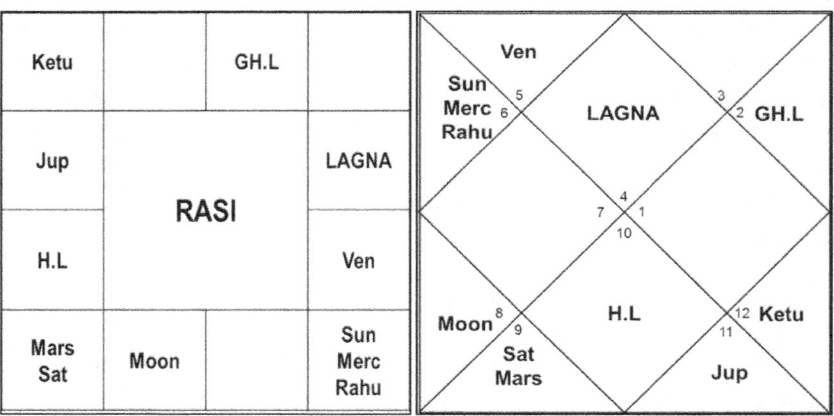

Compare the process of calculating the Ghatika Lagna in this example horoscope with that of example horoscope 1. Here, though the Lagna is an even sign Cancer, the Ghatika Lagna is determined by counting 47 Ghatis of birth time starting from Cancer in zodiacal order while the counting was done in anti-zodiacal order in example horoscope 1 for Lagna in Cancer. The only difference between the two Chakras is that Rahu is present in Lagna in example horoscope 1 while in the present horoscope the Lagna is not occupied by the nodes. Therefore, it becomes clear that the presence of a node in the Lagna necessitates the anti-zodiacal counting to determine the Ghatika Lagna. Otherwise, irrespective of the odd or even nature of the Lagna, the counting is to be carried out in zodiacal order only.

अत्र विलग्न इति प्राचीनवचनात् | श्रीः पत्नीलाभयोश्चेति |१|३|२२|| सूत्राच्चापि विशेषराजयोगः | तथा हि | लग्नं गुरुः पश्यति | सप्तमका.(ललग्नान् शुक्रःपश्य).ति || लग्नसप्तमकालान् चन्द्रः पश्यति | तथा च | गुरुशुक्रयोर्दृश्यन्यूनभूतयोरर्गळविषयत्वे | तदाधिक्याच्चन्द्रस्यैव योगद...यत्वम् | द्वितीयैकादशयोर्ग्रहबाहुल्यात् व्ययतृतीययोर्ग्रहाभावात् योगसहकारित्वं योगांतरकर्तृत्वं च | यद्यपि | चन्द्र......(के)तुर्वर्तते | तथापि | नन्यूना विबलाश्च ||१|१|८|| इति विपरीतफलकर्तृत्वं नास्ति |

As per the Vruddha Karika starting with **विलग्न**, and the Sutra **श्रीः पत्नीलाभयोश्चेति** |१|३|२२|| there is a special Raja Yoga forming in this Chakra. Jupiter aspects the Lagna while Venus aspects the Hora Lagna in the 7th house Capricorn. The Moon aspects the Lagna in Cancer, and the 7th house and Hora Lagna in Capricorn. Hence, as the Moon aspects more factors in comparison with Jupiter and Venus, the Moon would become the Yogada. Thus, the Argala Yogas are to be judged for the Moon. From the Moon, as the 2nd and 11th signs have many planets while the 12th and 3rd are unoccupied, this enhances and supports the Yoga and also forms another Yoga. Though.... there is Ketu from the Moon, it cannot cause reversal in the Yoga as per the Sutra **नन्यूना विबलाश्च** ||१|१|८||.

NOTES: The Vruddha Karika referred here is **विलग्नघटिकालग्नहोरालग्नानिपश्यति | एकग्रहोराजयोगो लग्नद्वयमथापिवा** |. In this case, among the three Lagnas, the Lagna is aspected by Jupiter and the Moon while the Hora Lagna is aspected by the Moon and Venus. No planet aspects the Ghatika Lagna in Taurus. Thus, as two Lagnas have planetary aspects a Raja Yoga is formed. Next, the Sutra **श्रीः पत्नीः लाभयोर्दृष्ट्या निराभासार्गळया** becomes applicable in this case. Among the aspecting planets, Jupiter aspects the Lagna, Venus aspects the Hora Lagna in the 7th house and the Moon aspects the Lagna, and Hora Lagna in the 7th house. For the purpose of Argala analysis, therefore, the Moon is to be considered to be the Yogada as per the Sutra **नन्यूना विबलाश्च** because, he aspects more factors than Jupiter and Venus. It can be noted here that this work assigns the term Yogada to a planet that becomes qualified for the Argala analysis as per the rules mentioned here.

When the Argala positions from the Moon are judged, the 2nd sign Sagittarius has two planets (Mars and Saturn) while the 11th sign Virgo has three planets (the Sun, Mercury and Rahu) forming strong Argalas. Their counter positions – the 12th sign Libra and the 3rd sign Capricorn – are unoccupied and hence incapable of producing Virodha Argala. Though Aquarius that happens to be a trine to the 12th house has Jupiter, the trines of the 2nd house have more number of planets. Hence, Virodha Argala will not form following the rule **नन्यूना विबलाश्च**. The placement of Jupiter in the 4th house in an Argala position appears to be cancelled by the placement of Venus in the 10th having more number of planets in its trines. Also, the placement of Ketu in a trine to the Moon should have caused reversal in the effect of Argala as per the rule **विपरीतं केतोः**. Unfortunately, we are clueless here because of the gap in the manuscript. Apparently, the strength of the Argala signs over the Virodha signs has ultimately resulted in the benefic influence of the aspecting planet Moon as per the rule **नन्यूना विबलाश्च**.

....कन्यादि प्रथमः खण्डः अष्टाविंशति वर्षः २८| मकरादि द्वितीयखण्डः | मकरस्य द्वादशवर्षाणि | आहत्य चत्वारिंशद्वर्षाणि ४० |......तदुपरि कुंभदशा एकादशवर्षा ११| अत्र भाग्याधिपगुरोर्विद्यमानत्वा....कालः | आहत्य एकपञ्चाशत् |

The first portion (of the Drik Dasa having four signs) will start from Virgo and has duration of 28 years. The second portion (of Drik Dasa) starts from Capricorn. The duration of Capricorn Dasa is 12 years. The cumulative age of the native by the end of Capricorn Dasa would be 40 years. This is followed by Aquarius Dasa of 11 years duration. As the 9th lord Jupiter is placed in Aquarius, the native will have a time (of great fortune and prosperity). The total years by the end of Aquarius Dasa are 51.

NOTES: The Drik Dasa has been taken from Virgo, the 9th sign from Capricorn. This might be because Capricorn as the 7th house is stronger than the Lagna Cancer. As the Lagna is not occupied by the nodes, the Dasa years of each Dasa sign are counted here following the rule **नाथांताः समाः प्रायेण** in zodiacal order irrespective of the odd and even nature of the Dasa sign. This is an important deviation from the method of Dasa year calculation mentioned in other works like Jataka Sara Sangraha. The first portion of the Drik Dasa consisting of the four signs Virgo, Libra, Scorpio and Sagittarius will be completed by the 28th year of the native. The duration of each of these signs are: Virgo Dasa – 12 years when counted in zodiacal order up to Venus, the planet placed immediately behind the Dasa sign Virgo occupied by its lord Mercury; Libra Dasa – 11 years when counted up to its lord Venus in zodiacal order; Scorpio – 2 years when counted up to its lord Mars in zodiacal order; Sagittarius – 3 years when counted up to its lord Jupiter in zodiacal order. This totals to a period of 28 years.

The second portion of the Drik Dasa consists of the four signs Capricorn, Aquarius, Pisces and Aries. The duration of Capricorn Dasa is of 12 years when counted up to its lord Saturn in zodiacal order. Hence, by the end of Capricorn Dasa the native would have completed 40 years (28 + 12) of age. The next Dasa of Aquarius will be for 11 years when counted up to its lord Saturn in zodiacal order. As the 9th lord from Lagna, Jupiter, is placed in Aquarius, the native will experience fortunate time during this period. By the end of Aquarius Dasa, the cumulative age of the native would be 51 years (40 + 11).

....तदुपरि मीनदशा द्वादशवर्षा १२। मीनाधिपगुरुस्थितकुंभात् नवमतुलादिखण्डः । .....तत्र तुलाखण्डस्य त्रिवर्षाणि । गुरुशुक्रदृष्ट्या शुभफलानि । तदुपरि वृश्चिककखण्डः त्रिवर्षः ३। अत्रभुक्तिःखण्डः ....विभज्य वृश्चिकमीनकर्कटेषु कल्पयेत्।

त्रिधाविभक्तांतु दशां त्रिकोणे – विकल्प्य तत्रस्थितखेचराणाम्। दशांनयेत् खेचरसंख्यया दा ....राशिफलेफलंस्यात्॥

The next Dasa of Pisces would be of 12 years duration. Taking the 9th house Libra from Aquarius, the sign occupied by Jupiter, the lord of Pisces Dasa....the duration of Libra quarter would be for 3 years. As Libra receives the aspect of benefics Jupiter and Venus, there will be benefic results in this quarter. The second quarter belonging to Scorpio will also be of 3 years. Here, the Bhuktis have to be divided into three parts and assigned to the trinal signs Scorpio, Pisces and Cancer as per the Vruddha Karika **त्रिधाविभक्तांतु दशां त्रिकोणे – विकल्प्य तत्रस्थितखेचराणां। दशांनयेत् खेचरसंख्यया दा ....राशिफलेफलंस्यात्॥.**

NOTES: The next Dasa of Pisces is of 12 years duration when counted up to its lord Jupiter in zodiacal order. The author applies the Khanda analysis to the Pisces Dasa which happens to be the 9th house from the Lagna. Readers are requested to note an important observation here. In the previous horoscope 2 and here also, the sign considered for Khanda analysis has 12 years duration besides being the 9th house from the Janma Lagna or the 7th house. Hence, the sign having a period of 12 years may be qualified for Khanda analysis as another criterion. The total duration of 12 years of Pisces Dasa is divided into four quarters of 3 years each. The first quarter is assigned to Libra, the 9th sign from the sign occupied by the Dasa lord Jupiter. As Libra is aspected by benefics Jupiter and Venus, this period of 3 years will give favourable results to the native. The next quarter of 3 years belong to the next sign Scorpio. Here, the author asks us to divide the duration of the quarter into three parts and assign them to the trines of the sign ruling over the quarter. Hence, after dividing the 3 years of Scorpio quarter into three parts, each part will get 1 year each. Therefore, Scorpio gets 1 year, Pisces gets 1 year and Cancer gets 1 year respectively.

अत्र वृश्चिके चन्द्रोपरिगुरुत्वात्प्रथमवर्षं शुभफलं | तदुपरिमीनवर्षे केतुसंबन्धात् कष्टफलं | तदुक्तं |.......न्नंशे क्रूरदशायां करोति वैकल्यमिति || अत्रमहान् क्लेशकालः | आहत्यवत्सराः ५६|

Here, as the Moon is present in Scorpio, the Dasa lord Jupiter attains exaltation and hence this period of Scorpio Bhukti of one year would give benefic results. The next year belonging to the Pisces Bhukti will cause difficulties as Pisces is occupied by malefic Ketu. In this connection it is said **|.......न्नंशे क्रूरदशायां करोति वैकल्यमिति ||**. Hence, the native will experience great mishaps in this Pisces Bhukti. The cumulative age of the native by the end of this Pisces Bhukti will be 56.

NOTES: The first 1 year of Scorpio will turn out to be fortunate as the Dasa lord Jupiter gets the exaltation effect because of the presence of the Moon, his exaltation sign lord, in Scorpio. The next 1 year of Pisces will give severe difficulties to the native as Pisces is occupied by malefic Ketu. By the end of Pisces part of the Scorpio quarter the native will complete his 56th year (by the end of Aquarius Dasa the native completed his 51st year. Adding 3 years of Libra quarter of Pisces Dasa, 1 year of Scorpio Bhukti of Scorpio quarter and 1 year of Pisces Bhukti of Scorpio quarter to 51 will give 56 years).

तदुपरि कर्कटकदशा एकवर्षा । अत्रापि क्लेशः । अशुभमवश्यं वाच्यम् । दशा.......नीचारिराशिगतानां पापानां विशेषेणेति ॥

The next Dasa (Bhukti) of Cancer is of one year. This period will also be full of difficulties as it is said **दशा.....नीचारिराशिगतानां पापानां विशेषेणेति ॥**.

NOTES: The next 1 year of Cancer also turns out to be unfavourable to the native because of the debilitation of its lord Moon who is also a malefic because of his Pakshabala.

धन्विखण्डस्त्रिवर्षः ३ । अत्रपापद्वयसंबन्धात् अधिकक्लेशकालः । अत्र कुजस्य अधिकभागत्वात् प्रथमखण्डः .....कष्टकालः ।

The next quarter of Sagittarius will be of 3 years. As Sagittarius is occupied by two malefic planets (Mars and Saturn) this quarter will also cause more difficulties to the native. Here, as Mars attains more degrees (than Saturn), the first part (of this quarter).....will be a difficult period.

NOTES: The next quarter after Scorpio belongs to Sagittarius. As it is occupied by two malefic planets Mars and Saturn, this period of 3 years would prove to be difficult for the native. However, the author mentions here another method of finding out the results of the quarter based on the degree-wise position of the planets placed in the sign. Here Mars being placed in the 26th degree has gained more degrees than Saturn who is placed in the 10th degree. Thus, the duration of the quarter is divided into two and the first part assigned to Mars while the second part is assigned to Saturn. The first part would give good results to the native while the second part would cause difficulties. The reasons for this are explained in the next lines.

एवं कैश्चिद्व्याख्यातं । मकरदशा चत्वारिंशद्वर्षा.....। तदुपरि कुंभदशाराह्वन्तसंख्यया अष्टवर्षा । तदुपरि मीनदशा (द्वा)दशवर्षेति । अस्मिन्पक्षे अष्टाचत्वारिंशदुपरि तुलाखण्डः त्रिवर्षः ।

Some scholars also opine in this manner... (up to) Capricorn Dasa would be 40 years. Later, the Dasa of Aquarius if counted up to Rahu will be of 8 years duration. This is followed by the Pisces Dasa of 12 years. In this case, after 48 years of the native the Libra quarter of 3 years duration will commence.

NOTES: Here, the author mentions the opinion of other scholars who consider Rahu as the lord of Aquarius in this case. What criteria they have considered for this purpose is not clear because of the gap in the manuscript. The Drik Dasa that started from Virgo would complete 40 years period by the end of Capricorn Dasa as explained before. Following the alternative opinion, the duration of Aquarius Dasa would be of 8 years when counted up to Rahu in zodiacal order. The next Dasa of Pisces is of 12 years as explained earlier. As per this view, the first quarter of Pisces Dasa ruled by Libra will start after the native completes his 48th year instead of 51st year as explained previously.

अत्र कुजस्य ग्रहक्रमात् प्राधान्यम् । तत्खण्डस्सार्धैकवर्षः । उच्चा ...रंभकालः । तदुपरिशनेःखण्डस्सार्धैकवर्षः । कुजोपरिशानेर्नीचत्वाच्छनेरुपरिगुरुदशासंबन्धादत्यंतनीचत्वेन बहुक्लेशकाल इत.....सप्तपञ्चाशत् । तदुपरिमीन(मकर)खण्डस्त्रिवर्षः । गुरोस्स्वभावनीचत्वेपि शुक्रचन्द्रदृष्ट्या यत्किंचित्सौख्यमिति तात्पर्यम् ।

Here, Mars will have preference as per the planetary sequence. That portion will be of one and half years. Exaltation…..starting period. Later, the portion of Saturn will be of another one and half years. As Saturn becomes debilitated with the association of Mars, and Jupiter, the Dasa lord, becomes debilitated with the association of Saturn, this period having the influence of two debilitated planets will turn out to be full of mishaps for the native…..the years will be 57. This is followed by the Capricorn quarter of 3 years duration. Though the Dasa lord Jupiter becomes debilitated in this sign by nature, because of the aspect of Venus and the Moon on Capricorn, there could be some comforts for the native.

NOTES: As explained earlier, Mars attains more degrees in Sagittarius and hence gains preference over Saturn. The 3 years duration of Sagittarius quarter is divided into two parts of 1½ years each. The first 1½ years of Mars would prove to be fortunate to the native as Mars attains exaltation position as he joins his exaltation sign lord Saturn in Sagittarius. The subsequent 1½ years would be highly problematic to the native as Saturn gets debilitation effect by joining his debilitation sign lord Mars in Sagittarius. This is further compounded by the fact that the Dasa lord Jupiter also gets debilitation effect in Sagittarius because of the presence of the lord of his debilitation sign - Saturn. Thus, the malefic influence of two debilitated planets would cause severe difficulties to the native in this period. The cumulative age of the native by the end of Sagittarius quarter would be 57 years (it was 48 years by the end of Aquarius Dasa. To this, add 3 years each of Libra, Scorpio and Sagittarius quarters. Thus, 48 + 9 will be 57 years). The next and last quarter of 3 years of Pisces Dasa is ruled by Capricorn. As the Dasa lord Jupiter attains debilitation effect in this sign by nature, this period too would give difficulties. However, there will also be some comforts to the native because of the aspect of Venus and Moon on Capricorn.

With this, the discussion about determining the Nidhyatu Yogada planet, Argala analysis and Drik Dasa interpretation comes to an end.

आत्माधिकः कलादिभिर्नभोगः सप्तानामष्टानां वा ||११||

इत्यारभ्य मन्दोज्यायान्गृहेषु ||१|१|..|| इत्यंतेन प्रकारेण चतुर्दशसूत्रात्मकेन आत्मकारकत्रयं च प्रदर्शितं | अय....भिरिति | हेतौ तृतीया | षष्ट्यंशरूपाभिः कलाभिः अधिकोग्रह आत्मा | अयमेकः |

By the 14 Sutras starting from the present Sutra **आत्माधिकः कलादिभिर्नभोगः सप्तानामष्टानां वा** ||११|| and ending with the Sutra **मन्दोज्यायान्ग्रहेषु** ||१|१|..||, the three types of Atma Karakas are explained. The planet attaining greater number of minutes among the 60 minutes of a degree is one of the three Atma Karakas.

NOTES: Though the author gives here the literal interpretation of the Sutra **आत्माधिकः कलादिभिर्नभोगः सप्तानामष्टानां वा** by mentioning that the planet that has gained greater number of minutes among the 60 minutes, he does not mean to suggest us to consider only the minutes to determine the Atma Karaka. By the subsequent discussions and also through the case studies, he used the degree-wise positions of planets first to determine the Atma Karaka, and only when two planets have attained same degree, he considers their minute-wise positions. He specifically mentions the term *Bhagakaladhika*, the one who attains greater degrees and minutes, to refer to the Atma Karaka planet.

कलाभिरक्षरसंख्यया सप्तभिः प्रकरणाद्ग्रहैर्हेतुभिरधिको.....पश्च | ग्रहपतित्वाद्रविरधिकः | विभावसुर्ग्रहपतिरित्यमराभिधानाच्च | अयं द्वितीयः आत्मा |

The word *Kalabhih* has a numerical value of 7 which refers to the seven planets. Thus the planet which is greatest among the seven planets, i.e. the Sun, is the second Atma Karaka. Because, the Sun is called as the lord of Planets or *Grahapati* in *Amarakosa* by this Shloka विभावसुर्ग्रहपतिः.

लग्नाधिपस्तु । ग्रन्थांतरे । लग्नस्य तदिति संबन्ध......मिनः पत्यादिसंज्ञेति कृतसंज्ञात्वात् । अधिकइति तृतीय आत्मा । एवं च आत्मकारकत्रयमुपपादितम् ।

The Lagna lord is the third Atma Karaka. In other texts it is said…… In this way the three Atma Karakas are proposed here.

NOTES: As per our author, there are three Atma Karakas – (i) the planet that has attained more number of degrees and minutes, (ii) the Sun, and (iii) the Lagna lord.

चक्रं तु । स्वांशचक्रं पदचक्रमुपपदचक्रंचेति त्रिविधम् । चतुर्थं ग्रहचक्रम् । तदुत्तरत्र प्रदर्श्यते । तदितरचक्रत्रयं निरूपयितुमाह । नभोगस्सप्ताष्टानां.....।

The Chakras are of three types – Svamsa Chakra, Pada Chakra and Upapada Chakra. The fourth Chakra is the Graha Chakra which will be explained later. To explain the first three kinds of Chakras, the Rishi says नभोगस्सप्ताष्टानां.....।.

NOTES: The Svamsa Chakra is prepared by using the Bhagakaladhika Atma Karaka. The Pada Chakra is prepared based on the Lagna lord while the Upapada Chakra is prepared using the 7th lord. The Sun becomes pivotal in the case of Graha Chakra.

अयमर्थः । नभ इति चत्वारिंशत् । भगणशोधने चत्वारि । चतुर्थकेन्द्रमितियावत् । द्वितीयांतं च । गच्छतीति गः । .....स्सु प्रत्ययः । सप्तेत्यत्र ६७ सप्तशेषात् सप्तमकेन्द्रं भवति । अष्टेत्यत्र दशमकेन्द्रमितिस्थितम् । षष्ट्यंतं च । ग इति प्रत्येकमभिसंबध्यते । चतुर्थगस्सप्तमगोऽष्टानां च इति । सप्तेति च द्वितीयान्तं । तदर्हमिति पाणिनीयनिर्देशात् । कृद्योगेऽपि । उभयत्र कर्मणि द्वितीया । अन्यत्र....क्षणा षष्टी ।

This means, the word *Nabha* has a numerical value of 40 which will give the remainder 4 after removing the multiples of 12. This indicates the 4th house, a Kendra. The statement ends with the Dwitiya Vibhakti. The word *Gah* indicates that 'he moves'. …pratyaya. The word *Sapta* has a numerical value of 67 which will yield 7 as the remainder after expunging the multiples of 12. This refers to the 7th house, a Kendra. Again, the word *Ashta* refers to the

10th house, a Kendra. This ends with Shashthi Vibhakti. The word '*Ga*' applies to each of the Kendras. It means 'he moves in the 4th, 7th and 10th houses'. The last statements of the paragraph deal with Sanskrit Grammar.

NOTES: I feel that the author has considered this Sutra as आत्माधिकः कलादिभिर्नभोगः सप्तानामष्टानां without वा.

अयमर्थः । सएवात्मा चतुर्थसप्तमदशमकेन्द्रगतो भवति । अत्रात्मशब्देन अधिकभागकल लग्नधिपश्च गृह्यते । स च लग्नाधिपतिस्सप्तमाधिपतिमुपलक्ष.......दिय्य चक्रप्रदर्शनार्थम् ।

The meaning of this statement is, the *Atma* (Karaka) will move in the *Kendras* in the 4th, 7th and 10th signs. Here, the word Atma refers to the planet that has attained greater number of degrees and minutes and also to the Lagna lord. The reference to the Lagna lord also implies the 7th lord….to demonstrate the various kinds of Chakras.

ननु षष्ट्यंशरूपाभिः कलाभिः अधिकोग्रह आत्मेति स्पष्टं । सएवोत्तरत्रानुषज्यताम् । रविलग्नाधिपत्योरस्मिन्प्रकरणेंतर्भावः कुतोवसीयतेति चेन्न । अत्रैव ग्रहचक्रनिरूपणम् ।

A question may be raised in this context. It is clear that the planet attaining greater number of minutes among the 60 minutes in a degree is called as Atma. He will be used in the subsequent Sutras also. However, how can we infer that the word Atma also applies to the Sun and Lagna lord in this context? As an answer, here comes the definition of Graha Chakra.

राजानौरविशीतगू इति प्राचीनवचनं च रवेरंतर्भावगमकम् । लग्नाधिपतेस्तु अस्मिन्नेवप्रकरणे यावदीशाश्रयं पदम् ॥१।१।२७॥ इत्यत्र अर्गळत्वमभ्युपगम्य पदं कल्पयन्तः । अमात्यानुचराद्देवताभक्तिः ॥१।४।४३॥ इत्यत्र सप्तमाधिपतेरमात्यत्वंमत्वा दे(वता भक्तिः)......विचारयंतश्चान्तर्भावे प्रमाणम् ।

As per the saying राजानौ रविशीतगू of the earlier scholars, the Sun is implied as the Atma. In connection to the Lagna lord being the Atma, in this very quarter there comes a Sutra यावदीशाश्रयं पदं ॥१।१।२७॥ where the method of determining the Pada is explained after the Argalas. Further, following the Sutra अमात्यानुचराद्देवताभक्तिः ॥१।४।४३॥, the 7th lord is accepted as the Amatya and he is used to determine the deities to which a native gets devoted to. Thus, these factors point out to the fact that the Sun, the Lagna lord and the 7th lord are implied in this context.

तद्वचनं तु । लग्नाल्लग्नपतिर्यावद्राशिसंस्थस्ततोग्र(गृ)हात् । तावानृषिभिरारूढः कथितस्सर्वथात्वि(ति । पद)..मारूढपर्यायं मन्यंते । तच्च पदाधिकारे स्पष्टं भविष्यति ।

The Vruddha Karika defining the Pada is **लग्नाल्लग्नपतिर्यावद्राशिसंस्थस्ततो ग्र(गृ)हात् । तावानृषिभिरारूढः कथितस्सर्वथात्वि(ति)** |. The word Arudha is considered as a synonym of Pada. The definition and use of Pada will become further clear in the section dealing with the Pada.

NOTES: This shows that our author subscribes to the school which does not use exceptional rules in determining the Padas.

सप्तमाधिपतेः पश्चाद्ग्रहो देवतेति वदन्तः सप्तमाधिपतेरमात्यत्वं मन्यन्त.......। चक्रं स्वांश चक्रवत् । पदोपपदाधिकारयोरपि प्रत्येकंचक्रमस्तीति तत्तदधिकारकल्पनया अवसीयते । अलमतिविस्तरेण ।

By considering the planet placed behind the 7th lord, the deity to which the native is devoted is found. Thus, the 7th lord is considered as the *Amatya*…this Chakra will be similar to the *Svamsa Chakra*. The discrete treatment of *Pada* and *Upapada* in their respective Adhikaras (sections/quarters) indicates that there are distinct Chakras for both *Pada* and *Upapada*. This extensive discussion will be stopped here.

NOTES: Please refer to the third Parichcheda of Jataka Sara Sangraha translated by me to have a detailed treatment of the subject of Upasana Yogas to know the deity a native will be devoted to.

अत्रेयंप्रक्रिया । अधिकभागकलमात्मानं तद्राशिद्वादशांशेकल्पयेत् ।....तत्पदं भवति । सप्तमाधिपतिं सप्तमा.......पतितावतिराशौ कल्पयेत् । तदुपपदंभवति । ततश्चायमर्थः । एतेत्रयश्च क्रमेण द्वादशांशरूपस्वांशपदोपपदानां केन्द्रेषु आत्मानो भवन्ति । एकैकाधिपएव तत्तत्केन्द्रचतुष्टये निवेशनीय इति ।

The method of preparing the three Chakras will be explained now. Take the planet which attained greater number of degrees and minutes as Atma and place him in the Dwadasamsa of the sign occupied by him……this forms the Pada. The 7th lord, from the 7th….put in so many signs away. This forms the Upapada. The meaning here is, the three Atmas (Karakas) will be placed in the Kendras from these three signs – the Svamsa defined by the Dwadasamsa, the Pada and the Upapada – respectively. This means, the same Atma is placed in all the four Kendras in their respective Chakras.

NOTES: For the first time in the Jaimini literature I have seen that the word Amsa has been interpreted as Dwadasamsa here as opposed to the Navamsa generally used by all the other scholars. The author gives his logic to support this interpretation while describing the example horoscope. Dwadasamsa is the 12th part of a sign and has a span of 2°.30' each in the sign of 30° span. The rulership of the 12 Dwadasamsas of every sign will start from the sign itself and move in zodiacal order ending with its 12th sign. In other words, the first Dwadasamsa belongs to the sign itself while the last Dwadasamsa belongs to its 12th sign.

एवं च सति एकैकेनैव चतुर्णां तत्तत्केन्द्राणां स्थि.........ष्टैरष्टभिरष्टौभावास्सिद्धा भवन्ति | तथा हि | भागकलाधिकमात्मकारकमारभ्य न्यूनभागकलाक्रमेण अष्टग्रहान् ज्ञात्वा प्रथमग्रह....द्वितीयतृतीयौ ततोन्यूनौद्वौ निवेशनीयौ | चतुर्थेतु सएवात्मानिवेशनीय इति | प्रागुक्त पञ्चमषष्ठयोस्तु चतुर्थपञ्चमौ ततोन्यूनभागौ निवेशनीयौ | एवं स्वांशचक्रं निरूपितम् |

Thus, after keeping the Atma in the four Kendras,…. the remaining eight planets will be placed in the remaining eight signs in the following way. The eight planets that attained lesser number of degrees and minutes than the Atma Karaka in descending order should be known first. In the 2nd and 3rd houses from the Atma Karaka, the first two planets from the eight should be placed. The 4th house will be occupied by the Atma Karaka himself. In the 5th and 6th signs, the next two planets are to be placed. In this way, the Svamsa Chakra will be prepared.

NOTES: This method of preparing Svamsa, Pada and Upapada Chakras is unique and unprecedented. At least, I came to know about this method for the first time in this version of Jyotih Pradeepika.

पदचक्रं तु | पदकेन्द्रेषु चतृषु लग्नपतिर्निवेशनीय इत्युक्तम् | अन्तरालेषु चतृषु द्व(त)दादिक्रमेण द्वौद्वौ निवेशनीयौ | तत्पदचक्रंभवति |

In the Pada Chakra, the Lagna lord is to be placed in the four Kendras of the Pada. In the intervening signs, other eight planets should be placed sequentially in the order they are placed from the Lagna lord in the Rasi Chakra. This forms the Pada Chakra.

उपपदचक्रं तु | सप्तमाधिपतिमारभ्य स्थितिक्रमेण द्वौद्वौ उपपदकेन्द्रान्तरालेषु कल्पनीयौ | तदुपपदचक्रंभवति |

In the Upapada Chakra, other planets should be placed in the intervening signs of the Upapada Kendras in the sequential order as they are placed in the Rasi Chakra starting from the 7th lord.

एवं चक्रत्रयं निरूपितं भवति । प्रयोजनं तु तत्तदधिकारे द्रष्टव्यम् । त .....(पञ्चम)नवमयोः कल्पनाकल्पनाभ्यां नित्यकेन्द्रगतस्तत्तदात्मकारकः उपजीव्यत्वाच्च तत्तदात्माश्रयत्वात् सर्वदा स्थितमुपजीव्यत्वं चारवशात् संभवतिचेत् राजयोगनिष्कर्षः ।

Thus, the way of preparing the three kinds of Chakras has been explained. The utility of these Chakras is to be understood from their respective sections. …considering the 5th and 9th houses, and the prepared and actual planets, and the *Upajeevyatva* with the respective Atma Karakas always placed in their Kendras, when happens as per the Rasi Chart, Raja Yoga will surely manifest.

NOTES: The application of these Chakras to determine the Raja Yoga in the Chakra is mentioned here. The Kalpita or prepared positions of the planets refers to the position of the planets as arranged in these three – Svamsa, Pada and Upapada – Chakras. The Akalpita or actual position of the planets refers to their Rasi Chakra positions. When the Bhagakaladhika Atma Karaka or the Lagna lord of the Svamsa and Pada Chakras that occupy the four Kendras form Upajeevyatva Yogas with the 5th and 9th signs from the Lagna, Raja Yoga is formed. For the Bhagakaladhika Atma Karaka, the planet next in position as per the degrees and minutes is the Amatya Karaka. For the Lagna lord, the 7th lord is the Amatya Karaka as per the discussion at Sutra 13 in the following pages. Hence, in case of the Upapada Chakra which is based on the 7th lord, the 7th lord is the Amatya of the Lagna lord and his position is to be treated as such. This part of the manuscript is difficult to interpret because of the gaps. However, putting up the information in bits and pieces from the related sections of the manuscript I have reached this understanding. The next two paragraphs are also related to this discussion. I am considering the word *Chara Vashat* as referring to the planetary positions in the Rasi Chakra instead of considering the meaning transit for *Chara*.

स ईष्टेबन्धमोक्षयोः ॥१२॥

अनेन सूत्रेण (पञ्चम)नवमा(भ्यां)द्राजयोगान् दर्शयति । स इति तन्त्रेणोपात्तं स इति यावत् । पूर्वोक्तास्त्रयः कारका इत्यर्थः । ईष्टे ईशत इत्यर्थः । बन्ध ...ति बन्धस्त्रिनवति । ९३। मोक्षः पञ्चषष्टिः

| ६५| भगणशोधनया नवपञ्चयोरित्युक्तम् | तयोराज्यभावरूपयोरेतेकारका ईशते ईश्वराभवन्ति | तत्पञ्चमनवमयोरूपजी.....योगप्रदा इतियावत् |

With this Sutra स ईष्टेबन्धमोक्षयोः ||१२||, the Rishi explains Raja Yogas from the 5th and 9th houses. Here the word *Sa* refers to the three Karakas explained previously. The word *Eeshte* means lordship. The word *Bandha* has a numerical value of 93 while the word *Moksha* has the numerical value of 65. After deducting the multiples of 12, they give 9 and 5 as remainders respectively. Thus, the three Karakas will act as the lords for causing Raja Yogas for.....This means, by becoming the *Upajeevyas* for the 5th and 9th....they bestow the Raja Yoga.

NOTES: The author asks us to consider the three Karakas mentioned previously. This would normally refer to the three Atma Karakas – Bhagakaladhika Karaka, Lagna lord and the Sun. However, usage of Graha Chakra is excluded in this Upajeevya Raja Yoga analysis. Hence, I feel we need to consider the Bhagakaladhika Karaka, Lagna lord and the 7th lord here as the three Karakas corresponding to the three - Svamsa, Pada and Upapada - Chakras.

उपजीव्यत्वं च पुरतःपश्चादेकराशौवा अव्यवधानेनावस्थानम् | उभयमूलयोगास्तु राजामात्ययोः परस्परोपजीव्यत्वेन | अन्येनाव्यवधानेन दोषः | एवम् | .....त्रयः | अमात्यमूलयोगास्तु तत्तदमात्यानामुक्तरीत्या तत्तत्कारकपञ्चमनवमोपजीव्यत्वे त्रयस्संपद्यंते | एतेषांमध्ये त्र्यादिसंभवे सिंहासनाधिपतयः | द्वयोस्संबन्धे मण्डलाधिपतयः | ....मात्रसंबन्धे राजसमाः | योगैकदेशसंबन्धे क्षुद्रप्रभवः | इतिरीत्या तारतम्यमालोचनीयम् |

The term *Upajeevya* refers to the position (of the Raja and Amatya?) in the same sign or ahead or behind from each other, without having any gap in between. The Yogas based on both the Raja and Amatya are formed when both of them are disposed as mutual *Upajeevyas*. When there is a gap in between them, it causes a blemish and destroys the Yoga. In this way, ...three Raja Yogas would be formed. The Yogas based on the *Amatyas* will be formed when the *Amatyas* are placed in the 5th or 9th houses with their respective *Karakas* in the *Upajeevya* way explained above and they are also three in number. Among these Yogas, when three Yogas are formed, the native will become a *Simhasanadhipati* (ruler of an empire or kingdom). If two Yogas are formed, the native will be a *Mandaladhipati* (ruler of a smaller kingdom). ...when it/they have the association only, the native will be equal to a ruler. When only a single Yoga is formed, the native will be a *Kshudra Prabhu* (ruler of a very small region).

NOTES: Here, using the relative positions of the Atma and Amatya Karakas in the Svamsa, Pada, Upapada and Rasi Chakras with reference to the 5th and 9th house from the Janma Lagna, a total of six Raja Yogas are mentioned. Among them, if three or more Yogas are present in the Chakra, the native will become a king or emperor. If two Yogas are present he will become a Mandaladhipati. If only one Yoga is formed, the native will be a petty king or head of a small region.

There is a mention of an association which makes the native only an equivalent to a ruler but not a ruler directly. This means, the native will be wealthy and influential but not a king. In my opinion this Yoga will be formed when one of the planets is placed in a sign ahead or behind in the Upajeevya Yoga with reference to the 5th or 9th houses from the Janma Lagna. When the Karakas are in the same sign in the 5th or 9th house they form the said Raja Yogas in the hierarchy. This becomes clear when we study the example horoscopes.

The probability for the number of Yogas mentioned here is quite hard to understand. Considering the multitudes of Atma Karakas, Amatya Karakas, four kinds of Chakras including the Rasi Chakra, 5th and 9th house positions there are possibilities of formation of many number of Yogas. If we stick to the respective Atma Karakas and Amatya Karakas only, there can be some reduction in their numbers. However, the example horoscopes do not indicate usage of corresponding Atma and Amatya Karakas only.

तस्यानुसरणादमात्यः ||१३||

अत्रापि तन्त्रेणग्रहणम् | तस्य तस्येत्यर्थः | अनुसरणादित्यत्र....स्यानंतर्यमनुसरणम् | ततश्च तत्समनंतरं न्यूनभागकलः तं प्रत्यमात्यः |

Here also, *Tasya* means the Karaka. *Anusaranam* means following from behind. Hence, the planet having immediately lesser degrees and minutes than the Karaka is the Amatya.

रवेस्तु अनुसरणंपुरतः पश्चाच्चावसर्पणम् | ततश्चन्द्रस्य पौर्णिमासीतःअमावास्यान्तं | अमावास्यातः पौर्णमास्यंतं....ति | स एव रवेरमात्यः | यद्वा ग्रहचक्रे रवेरनन्तरं चन्द्रइति तदनुसरणादमात्यत्वम् |

In the case of the Sun, following happens in the front and moving away happens behind. It means, the Moon follows the Sun from *Purnima* (full moon) to *Amavasya* (new moon), and from *Amavasya* to *Purnima* the Moon moves away from the Sun. Thus, the Moon is the *Amatya* for the Sun. Otherwise, as the Moon comes after the Sun in the Graha Chakra the Moon becomes the *Amatya* of the Sun.

Here, we are informed that the Moon is Amatya Karaka when the Sun is considered as the Atma Karaka. However, apparently they are not considered in the analysis of Upajeevya Raja Yogas as evident from the last three example horoscopes.

लग्नाधिपतेस्तु सप्तमाधिपतिरमात्यः | कथमितिचेत् अनुसरणमभिमुखीकृत्यसंचारः | स च सप्तमांशे लग्नं प्र.....भवतीति एषामितिभावः | तद्वारा सप्तमाधिपतेरमात्यत्वं | एवममात्यास्त्रयो दर्शिताः | राजयोगार्थममात्यत्वकल्पनम् | तद्यथा | रवेराजयोगकारकत्वम् |

For the Lagna lord, the 7th lord will be the *Amatya.* How is this? Because, *Anusarana* also means moving in front of someone. This means, the 7th lord in the Saptamamsa moves……in relation to Lagna…..this happens to the Lagna lord and the 7th lord. Thus, the 7th lord becomes *Amatya* for the Lagna lord. In this way, the three *Amatyas* are explained. *Amatyas* are used to determine the Raja Yogas in a horoscope – like, the Sun stands as a significator for Raja Yoga.

NOTES: To justify the 7th lord as the Amatya Karaka for the Lagna lord the author seemingly refers to the Saptamamsa among the Vargas. Saptamamsa is the 7th part of a sign. In odd signs the seven Saptamamsas belong to the seven signs starting from the sign itself ending with its 7th sign while in an even sign they belong to the seven signs starting from its 7th sign ending with the sign under consideration. Thus, at any given point, the Saptamamsas of any two opposing signs (mutually seventh signs) belong to mutually seventh signs. For example, the 1st Saptamamsa of Aries belongs to Aries while the 1st Saptamamsa of Libra belongs to Libra. The 2nd Saptamamsa of Aries belongs to Taurus while the 2nd Saptamamsa of Libra belongs to Scorpio. Hence, the 7th lord is considered as the Amatya for the Lagna lord.

तस्य भ्राता ||१४||

तस्य तृतीय ....भागकलाधिकस्य भागक्रमेण तृतीयो भ्राता | रवेस्तु द्वितीयश्चन्द्रः तृतीयः कुज इति तस्य भ्रातृत्वम् | लग्नाधिपतेस्तृतीयाधिपतिर्भ्राता | एवं चक्रत्रयेऽपि सप्तमपर्यन्तं स ......शास्त्रांतरप्रसिद्धमेव-कारकत्वमुपदिष्टम् | तथा हि | अंशचक्रे पदचक्रे च प्रागुक्तरीत्या सप्तमान्तं वेदितव्यम् | ग्रहचक्रेतु रविः प्रथमः चन्द्रो द्वितीयः | कुजस्तृतीयः | बुधश्चतुर्थः | स एव मातृकारकः | गुरुः पञ्चमः | स एव पुत्रकारकः | एतावता प्रसिद्ध्यानुपूर्विकाकारकत्वं सिद्धमेव |

The third planet as per the position of decreasing degrees and minutes from the Karaka is the *Bhrata* (brother). In the case of the Sun, the third planet in the sequence, Mars, happens to be the Karaka for brothers. In the case of the Lagna lord, the 3rd lord will be the *Bhrata.* In this way, in the three Chakras (Svamsa Chakra, Pada Chakra and Graha Chakra) the Karakas up to the 7th Karaka are to be determined……the same Karakas that are mentioned in other well-known treatises are also mentioned here. Thus, in the Svamsa Chakra and Pada Chakra, the seven Karakas are to be determined as explained before. In the Graha Chakra, the Sun happens to be the first Karaka. The Moon is Karaka for the second, Mars for the third, and Mercury for the fourth. Mercury is thus the Matru Karaka also. Jupiter is the fifth Karaka and hence the Karaka of sons. Up to this point in the sequence, the noted significations of planets are quite familiar.

NOTES: The different Karakas to be considered for different Chakras is explained here up to the 7th house. It is said that in the case of Svamsa Chakra, the seven planets in descending order of their longitudes will form the seven Karakas. However, there is a discrepancy here. As the author considers Rahu also, there are eight Karakas in total.

In the case of Pada Chakra also, we are asked to consider the 3rd lord as the Bhratru Karaka. Similarly, we have to consider the 4th, 5th and 6th lords as Matru, Putra and Jnati Karakas respectively. However, the 7th lord is considered as Amatya Karaka instead of Kalatra Karaka while the Karakatva of the 2nd lord remains unclear. Thus, there is a discrepancy here and unfortunately we don't receive any help from the manuscript in present condition.

Instead of considering the planets as the Karakas, if we consider the respective houses in the respective Chakras there will not be any discrepancy. However, here also a problem will arise as the respective Atma Karakas are placed in the four Kendras in the Chakras as we see further.

तस्य माता ||१५|| तस्य पुत्रः ||१६||

इति सूत्रद्वयेन प्रसिद्धमेवानूद्यते |

With these two Sutras, the well-known significations are repeated.

तस्य ज्ञातिः ||१७||

शनिः | तदनंतरं शुक्रः | शनेः ज्ञातिकारकत्वम् |

Here, Saturn comes first followed by Venus. Saturn becomes Jnati Karaka, or the significator for the enemies.

तस्य दाराश्च ||१८||

शुक्रस्य दारकारकत्वम् | गुरुशुक्रशशनिरिति ग्रहानुपूर्विकैवदर्शिता | आसप्तमांतं प्रसिद्धमेव कारकत्वमुपपादितम् |

Venus becomes the *Dara Karaka*, the significator for wife. The sequence of Jupiter, Venus and Saturn itself has been mentioned here in a slightly different fashion. Thus, the well-known significations of planets up to the seventh Karaka are explained.

मात्रासहपुत्रमेके समामनन्ति ||१९||

मात्रा पञ्चषष्टिः ६५| भगणशेषात् पञ्चमेन | पुत्रं २१ भगणशेषात् नवममित्यर्थः | एके समामनंति | कथयन्तीति | पुत्रकारकस्यैव पितृकारकत्वमिति |

Matra has a numerical value of 65 while *Putra* has a value of 21. After deducting the multiples of 12, they give 5 and 9 as remainders. Thus, this Sutra says that some scholars take the *Putra Karaka* (Karaka for sons) himself as the *Pitru Karaka* (Karaka for father).

NOTES: Generally, the interpretation of this Sutra is – Matru Karaka is also considered as the Putra Karaka by few scholars. However, our author applies the Katapayadi system here and derives the meaning that few scholars want to consider Putra Karaka as the Pitru Karaka also.

अष्टमादिव्ययान्तानां प्रसिद्धमेवसा ......(स्वांश)चक्रपदचक्रयोर्वेदितव्यम् | अष्टमे निधनं मृत्युः | नवमेन गुरुर्धर्मश्च | दशमेन आज्ञा कर्म च | लाभेन लाभः | व्ययेन व्यय इति |

….from the eighth to the twelfth (houses?), the well-noted significations of….should be known in the Svamsa Chakra and Pada Chakra. The eighth stands for *Nidhana* or *Mrutyu* (death). The ninth stands for *Guru* (preceptor) and *Dharma* (religious merit), tenth for *Ajna* (executive power/position) and *Karma* (work or job), eleventh for *Labha* (gains) and the twelfth house stands for *Vyaya* (expenses).

NOTES: We are asked to consider the Bhavas from the 8th to 12th houses in the Svamsa Chakra and Pada Chakra to deal with these significations. The significations in the Graha Chakra are separately mentioned in the next five Sutras.

भगिन्यारतः श्यालः कनीयान् जननीचेति ||२०||

ग्रहचक्रे अष्टमादि पञ्चसुभावेषु पञ्चभिस्सूत्रैः कारकानाह | आरतइतिविंशतिः २०| अक्षरसंख्यया भगणशुद्धौ अष्टमत्वमापन्नात् आरतः कुजादित्यावृत्तिः | अस्मात् भगिनी-जननी-श्यालः-कनीयानिति चत्वारोवेदितव्याः | तेषाव......रक इत्यर्थः | एवं कुजेनाष्टमभाव उपपादितः ||

Now the Rishi mentions the Karakas for the five houses starting from the 8th house to the 12th house in the Graha Chakra. The word *Ara* has a numerical value of 20 which becomes 8 after deducting 12 and hence indicates the 8th house. The word *Ara* also means Mars, thus repeating the Karakatvas of Mars (earlier Mars has been given the Karakatva over 3rd house). Hence, from the 8th house and Mars the four relatives - one's sisters, mother, younger brother of one's wife, own younger brothers – are to be judged. This means …is the Karaka. In this way, the 8th house has been attributed to Mars.

NOTES: We can note here that the Karakas from Mars to Venus attributed to the 3rd house to the 7th house are repeated again from the 8th house to the 12th house.

मातुलादयो बान्धवा मातृसजातीया इत्युत्तरतः ||२१||

उत्तरतः अष्टमात्परतः नवमत्वमापन्नात् उत्तरतः ......रतो बुधात् | अत्राप्यावृत्तिः | अयमर्थः | मातुलादयोमातृसजातीया बान्धवः बुधेन ज्ञातव्याः | एवं बुधेन नवमो दर्शितः | पूर्वसूत्रमारभ्य अं.....त्यंतेषु चतृषुसूत्रेषु इति करणमिदमर्थः तत्पञ्चम्यर्थेन संबध्यते | तदेवावृत्ति गमकम् | ततश्चैवमर्थोभवति | आरादित्यस्मात् आरादष्टमादित्यस्मात् कुज.......पूर्वसूत्रार्थः | अत्रतु उत्तरतइत्युत्तरतः नवमादित्येवं रूपात् बुधात् इत्यर्थः | उत्तरत्रोप्येवंज्ञेयम् | सर्वत्रावृत्तिपरयोश्शब्दयोः भावपरशब्दो विशेषणं ग्रहपरशब्दो विशे.......||

Uttaratah means from the next sign after the 8th house, i.e. the 9th house. And, from the next planet after Mars, i.e. from Mercury.

Here also there is repetition of Karakatvas (Mercury has been given the Karakatva over the 4th house). The next discussion is about the Sanskrit grammatical rules which explain the repetition of the planets and reference to the houses and planets.

पितृपितामहौ पतिपुत्राविति गुरुमुखादेव जानीयात् ||२२||

अत्र गुरुः त्रयोविंशतिः २३| भगणशोधनया एकादश इति गम्यते | तस्यमुखात् प्रारंभात् दशमादितियावत् ||.......योजनीयः | ततश्चायमर्थः | गुरुमुखात् दशमत्वमापन्नात् गुरुमुखात् तस्मादेव प्रधानादितियावत् | मुखंप्रधानत्वमित्यमरः | प्रकृते कारकादितिपर्यवसति | तस्माज्जीवात् पितामह प्रपितामहौ .....र्थः | पतिस्स्वामी | पुत्रः प्रसिद्धः | तेषामयंकारक इति यावत् | एवं दशमभावो गुरुणा दर्शितः |

Here, the word *Guru* has a numerical value of 23 which gives 11 as remainder after deduction of 12. The word *Mukha* means at the beginning. Thus, the house at the beginning of 11, i.e. 10th house, is indicated by the word *Guru Mukhat*. Further, *Mukhat* also means primarily as per the statement of *Amarakosa* **मुखंप्रधानत्वं**. Thus from Jupiter, primarily the native's grandfather and great-grandfather.......*Pati* means husband or lord. *Putra* has a well-known meaning referring to sons. For these relatives, Jupiter is the Karaka. Thus, the 10th house has been attributed to Jupiter.

पत्नीपितरौ श्वशुरौ मातामहौ इत्यंतेवासिनः ||२३||

अन्तेवासिन इत्यक्षरसंख्यया .....द्वादशशेषाल्लग्नादारभ्य अन्तेवासिनोभावादितिवा | द्वादशभावो गम्यते | तथाभूतांतेवासिनः गुरुसमीपवर्तिनः शुक्रादितियावत् | इदंचावृत्यालभ्यते | तथा च सति द्वादशभाव.......शुक्रात् पत्नी भार्या श्वशुरौ तत्पितरौ | पितरौ आत्मनो मातापितरौ आत्मनो मातामहीमातामहश्च एते विचारणीया इत्यर्थः | दशमानन्तरं द्वादशभावनिरूपणम् | ग्रहाणां ....दिति वेदितव्यम् ||

As per the numerical value the word '*Anta*' of *Antevasina*.....as 12 remains as the remainder, or the house which comes last by counting from the Lagna, the 12th house is referred here. In case of the planets, *Antevasin* indicates the one living near to the *Guru* (Jupiter or preceptor) which is Venus. This Karakatva of Venus also shows repetition (Venus has been assigned the Karakatva of the 7th house). Thus, from Venus and the 12th house one's wife, in-laws, one's own parents, own maternal grandparents are to be judged. This Karakatva of the 12th house is explained after the 10th house Karakatvas. This is to be understood as....of the planets.

मन्दो ज्यायान् गृहेषु ॥२४॥

गृहेषु राशिरूपेषु भावेष्वितियावत् | मन्दश्शनिः | अक्षरसंख्यया एकादशो भावः | तेनच ज्यायान् ज्येष्ठभ्राता .....इत्यर्थः | गृहेषु अक्षरसंख्यया एकादशस्थाने मन्दोनिवेशनीयः | तेनच ज्यायान् ज्येष्ठभ्राता विचारणीयः |

Here, the word *Gruheshu* refers to the houses defined by the signs. *Manda* is another name of *Shani*. As per the numerical value, the word *Gruha* gives a remainder of 11 after deducting multiples of 12. Hence, it means that from Saturn and the 11th house one's elder brothers….As per the numerical value of the word *Gruheshu*, Saturn is to be placed in the 11th. From them (11th house and Saturn), the matters related to the elder brothers of the native are to be judged.

अत्राष्टमादारभ्य आद्वादशान्तं कुजबुधगुरु.....क्रमेण विन्यासात् पूर्वार्धेऽपि रविचन्द्रकुजबुधगुरुशनिशुक्राणां लग्नादारभ्य सप्तमांतं विन्यास इति ग्रहक्रमो दर्शितः | एवं ग्रहचक्रम् | अस्य प्रयोजनं ....ग विचारः | तेन तत्तद्भावारिष्टनिरूपणं दशाकल्पनया कालज्ञानंचेत्यादिद्रष्टव्यं |

Thus, the sequential placement of planets in the form of Mars, Mercury, Jupiter, Saturn and Venus in the latter half from the 8th house to the 12th house, and also the placement of the Sun, the Moon, Mars, Mercury, Jupiter, Saturn and Venus in the former half starting from the Lagna and ending with the 7th house has been explained. This is known as the *Graha Chakra*. This is utilized in…..From that, the judgment of unfortunate events of the respective Bhavas and timing of such events by using the Dasas ought to be carried out.

NOTES: The Graha Chakra mentioned here with the planetary positions – Sun, Moon, Mars, Mercury, Jupiter, Saturn, Venus, Mars, Mercury, Jupiter, Saturn, and Venus – appears to be different from the Graha Chakra erecting method explained for the example horoscopes. Apparently, this Graha Chakra is used to predict the Arishtas (dangers) to the respective relatives of the native and to derive the Dasa to time the calamitous events. Unfortunately, the manuscript has gaps at an important point here where the utility of these Karakas in the Graha Chakra are mentioned.

EXAMPLE HOROSCOPE-4

अत्रोदाहरणम् | रामचन्द्रस्य जननम् | शकाब्दाः १५२९ | प्लवसंवत्सर ज्येष्ठमासं तेदि ९ उदयादि जननकालघटिकाः १४ | ०| लग्नं | ४|२|४२|| स्फुटग्रहाः | रविः | २|७|~~४७~~(२७?)|| चन्द्रः |

११|११|१८|| कुजः |२|१९|२९|| बुधः | १|१८|७|| गुरुः | ११|१८|५६|| शुक्रः |३|५|१०|| शनिः |८|२३|४६|| राहुः | ~~२~~(४)|१९|४||

An example will be presented now. The native named Ramachandra was born in the lunar year Plava corresponding to the Saka year 1529, on the 9th day of the month of Jyeshtha, 14 Ghatis after the sunrise. The longitudes of the Lagna and the nine planets are: Lagna - 4.02°.42', the Sun - 2.07°.~~47~~(27)', the Moon - 11.11°.18', Mars - 2.19°.29', Mercury - 1.18°.07', Jupiter - 11.18°.56', Venus - 3.05°.10', Saturn - 8.23°.46', and Rahu – ~~2~~(4).19°.04'.

Jup Moon		Merc	Mars Sun
Ketu BH.L	RASI		Ven
			LAGNA Rahu
Sat			

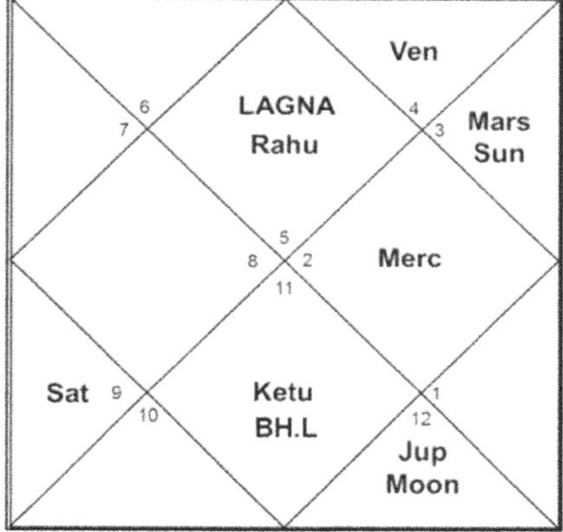

NOTES: As per the details given here, the native was born between 17th and 18th of June, 1607 AD matching with the Hindu calendar Plavanga Samvatsara Jyeshtha Bahula Ashtami and Navami respectively. The position of the Moon matches for 17th while that of the Sun matches for 18th. The time of birth would be approximately 10.40 AM.

अत्र स्वांश इति सामान्योक्तावपि द्वादशा...श्चैव न्यायम् | राशीनां द्वादशत्वात् | प्रदेशेषु | पञ्चमूषिकमार्जारा इत्यारभ्य उच्चेधर्मनित्यताकैवल्यंच ||१|२|१३|| इत्येतेषु द्वादशानां उपयोगदर्शनात् | यत्रयत्र विशेषोक्तैः होरादयः करणम् |..||.....|| इति | न तत्रतत्र तस्य ग्रहणम् |

Here, though the general word *Svamsa* has been used it indicates *Dwadasa(msa)*....as per the rule. This is because the signs are 12 in number. Further, in the forthcoming 12 Sutras starting from **पञ्चमूषिकमार्जारा** and ending with **उच्चे धर्मनित्यता कैवल्यंच**, the results of placement in the 12 signs have been explained. Wherever the usage of other Vargas like Hora and so on is specifically mentioned…..in those places this should not be considered.

NOTES: The author explains why he considers Dwadasamsa here for the word *Amsa* in the Sutra अथ स्वांशो ग्रहाणां. As the results of the Atma Karaka placed in the 12 signs from Aries to Pisces are explained in the Sutras from पञ्चमूषिकमार्जारा to उच्चे धर्मनित्यता कैवल्यंच, the author seems to opine that each Rasi should have the chance of the Atma Karaka to fall in one of the 12 Amsas for the results of the 12 Sutras to be applied. Hence, he takes Dwadasamsa instead of Navamsa. Further, he says that wherever the context demands the consideration of Hora and other Vargas, the word Amsa should be interpreted accordingly, but Dwadasamsa should not be considered there.

प्रकृते भागकलाधिकः शनिः | तस्य द्वादशांशः कन्या | तत्रशनिं कल्पयित्वा द्वितीये तुलायां तदनन्तरभागकलः कुजः | तृतीये वृश्चिके तदनन्तरो राहुः | चतुर्थे धनुषि शनिः | पञ्चमे मकरे राहुसमः केतुः | कुंभे षष्ठे तदनन्तरभागकलो गुरुः | सप्तमे शनिः | अष्टमे मेषे बुधः | नवमे तदनन्तरभागकलश्चन्द्रः | दशमे मिथुने शनिः | एकादशे कर्कटे चन्द्रानन्तरभागो रविः | द्वादशे सिंहे तदनन्तरभागकलं शुक्रं कल्पयेत् |

In this horoscope, Saturn happens to be the *Bhagakaladhika* (planet having attained greatest number of degrees and minutes among the 9 planets). The *Dwadasamsa* of Saturn happens to be Virgo. Hence, in the *Svamsa Chakra*, Saturn is to be placed in Virgo. In the 2nd to Saturn, the next planet as per the degrees and minutes, Mars, is to be placed in Libra. The next planet Rahu is to be placed in Scorpio in the 3rd to Virgo. In the 4th house, a Kendra, again Saturn is to be placed. In the 5th sign from Virgo, Ketu, who has the same longitude as of Rahu, is to be placed in Capricorn. The next planet as per the position of degrees and minutes is Jupiter who should be placed in Aquarius in the 6th. In the 7th, a Kendra, again the Karaka Saturn is to be placed. In the 8th in Aries, the next planet Mercury is to be placed followed by the Moon in the 9th in Taurus. In the 10th in Gemini, a Kendra, again the Karaka Saturn is to be placed. In Cancer, the 11th from Virgo, the Sun who follows the Moon in degrees and minutes, is to be placed. Finally, in Leo in the 12th, the next planet Venus is to be placed. This forms the Svamsa Chakra.

NOTES: Note that the longitudes of Rahu and Ketu are considered as-it-is, not in the reverse order from the end of the sign they occupy. Rahu is considered first and Ketu, who has the same longitude is placed in the next possible sign in the Svamsa Chakra.

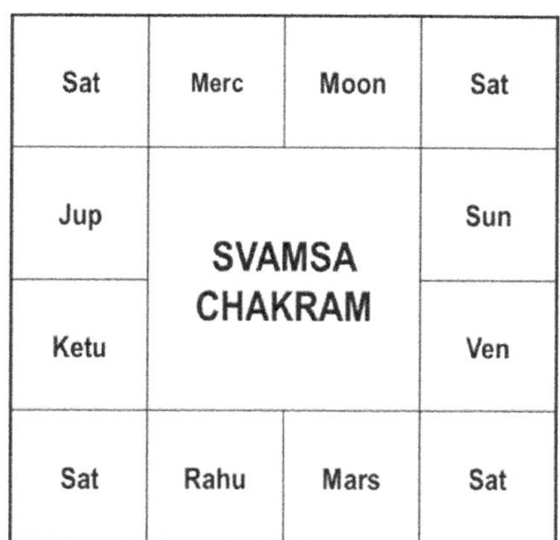

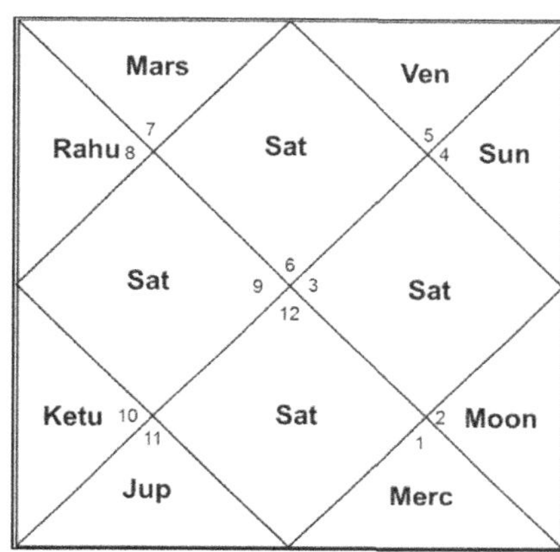

तस्य तस्य स्फुटभागकलयोः कल्पितराशावेव द्वादशांश कल्पनं | तत्तद्द्वादशांशमारभ्य ओजयुग्मन्यायेन अंशाद्दि(धिप)संख्यया दशावर्षानयनम् | एवं च सति प्रकृतेजातके शनेः पञ्च प्रथमः | ततः कुजस्यैकादश | ततोराहोर्द्वादश | ततःशनेः पञ्च | ततःकेतो राहोर्द्वादशात् सप्तमं धनुरवेक्ष्य चत्वारि | गुरोः पञ्च | ततः शनेश्चत्वारि | ततो बुधस्य षट् | ततश्चन्द्रस्य पञ्च | ततश्शनेरेकादश |

Next, consider the degrees and minutes of the planets omitting their signs to determine the Dwadasamsa they attain in their respective signs of Svamsa Chakra. Considering the Dwadasamsa sign attained by the planets, the Dasa years are to be counted following the odd and even nature of the signs. Thus, the duration of the first Dasa of Saturn is 5 years. The next Dasa of Mars is of 11 years. The duration of the next Dasa of Rahu is 12 years followed by the Saturn Dasa of 5 years. As the Dasa of Rahu turns out to be 12 years when counted from his Dwadasamsa sign Gemini, the next Dasa of Ketu when counted from its 7th sign Sagittarius would be of 4 years. The next Dasa of Jupiter is of 5 years. The next Dasa of Saturn is of 4 years followed by 6 years of Mercury Dasa. The next Dasa of the Moon is of 5 years. This is followed by the Saturn Dasa of 11 years.

NOTES: The method of deriving Dasa years is explained here based on the position of planets in the Svamsa Chakra. Ignoring the actual sign a planet occupies, consider the sign it occupies in the

Svamsa Chakra and determine the resultant Dwadasamsa sign of that Svamsa sign based on the degrees and minutes of the planet. After this, the duration of years of the planet Dasa is determined by counting from the resultant sign to the sign occupied by its lord (in the Rasi Chakra) following the zodiacal or reverse order based on the odd or even nature of the sign. Only for the first Dasa of the Atma Karaka, his actual position in the Rasi Chakra is to be considered to find out the resultant Dwadasamsa sign.

Planet	Deg & Min	Svamsa Sign	Dwadasamsa Sign	Dasa Years
Saturn	23°.46'	Virgo	Virgo	5
Mars	19°.29'	Libra	Taurus	11
Rahu	19°.04'	Scorpio	Gemini	12
Saturn	23°.46'	Sagittarius	Virgo	5
Ketu	19°.04'	Capricorn	Leo/Sagittarius	4
Jupiter	18°.56'	Aquarius	Virgo	5
Saturn	23°.46'	Pisces	Sagittarius	4
Mercury	18°.07'	Aries	Scorpio	6
Moon	11°.18'	Taurus	Cancer	5
Saturn	23°.46'	Gemini	Pisces	11
Sun	07°.27'	Cancer	Virgo	5
Venus	05°.10'	Leo	Libra	10

In the present case, the Atma Karaka Saturn is placed in Sagittarius in the Rasi Chakra and attains Virgo Dwadasamsa. As Virgo is an even sign, the duration of Saturn Dasa will be of 5 years when counted up to Mercury in anti-zodiacal order from Virgo. The next Dasa is of Mars placed in Libra in the Svamsa Chakra. Mars attains 19°.29' in Gemini in the Rasi Chakra. Ignoring the sign Gemini and considering the degrees and minutes of Mars in Libra, the Dwadasamsa sign attained by Mars is Taurus. Thus, Mars Dasa would be of 11 years when counted from Taurus to its lord Venus in anti-zodiacal order because Taurus is an even sign. In the same way, the next Dasa of Rahu who is placed in Scorpio in Svamsa Chakra will be of 12 years since he attains the Dwadasamsa of Gemini. The next Dasa of Saturn placed in Sagittarius in Svamsa Chakra will be of 5 years duration as he attains the Dwadasamsa of Virgo. In the case of next Dasa of Ketu there is an exception. Instead of taking the Dwadasamsa sign of the sign occupied by Ketu in Svamsa Chakra, the 7th sign from the sign considered for

Rahu is used. Hence, as Gemini was considered for Rahu Dasa, its 7th sign Sagittarius is to be considered for Ketu Dasa. The duration of Ketu Dasa would therefore be of 4 years. The next Dasa of Jupiter placed in Aquarius in Svamsa Chakra will be of 5 years duration as he attains the Dwadasamsa of Virgo. This is followed by the Dasa of Saturn placed in Pisces in Svamsa Chakra which has the duration of 4 years as Saturn attains the Dwadasamsa of Sagittarius. The next Dasa of Mercury placed in Aries in the Svamsa Chakra is of 6 years duration as Mercury attains the Dwadasamsa of Scorpio. Subsequent Dasa is of the Moon who is placed in Taurus in the Svamsa Chakra. This Dasa is of 5 years as the Moon attains the Dwadasamsa of Cancer. The next Dasa of Saturn placed in Gemini in Svamsa Chakra will be of 11 years duration. The reason behind this calculation is explained next.

ननु चतुर्थे(र्थो?)शनिर्मिथुनेकल्पितः | ततः आरभ्य शनिभुक्तद्वादशांशैर्दशभिः मीनस्यप्रसंगः | तत्रैव स्फुटगुरुर्वर्ततइति नाथांतास्समाः ||१|१|२८|| इत्येतत्सूत्रं न प्रवर्तते | सत्यं | प्रायेणेतिवचनात् अस्यास्तादृशाअपि समास्संभवन्ति | अत्रोपदेशः | ग्रहे स्वराशौसति ओजयुग्मन्यायेन पश्चाद्ग्रहांतसंख्यया वर्षानयनम् | ततश्शने.......स्य शनेरेकादशेति सुष्ठूक्तम् |

A question can be asked here. The fourth Saturn in Gemini has attained 10 Dwadasamsas which involve Pisces to determine the Dasa years. The lord of Pisces, Jupiter, occupies Pisces itself. Does the Sutra **नाथांतास्समाः** not applicable here? Yes, it is true. The Sutra does not apply here. Because of the word **प्रायेण** *Prayena*, such variations in calculation of Dasa years also happen. Here, the method of calculating the Dasa years will be explained. When a sign lord is placed in the sign itself, following the odd and even rule, the Dasa years are to be determined by counting to the planet immediately placed behind the sign. Hence, ……the 11 years of Dasa attributed to Saturn in Gemini is perfectly correct.

NOTES: Here, the author explains the exceptional rule to determine the Dasa years when the sign lord is placed in the sign itself. Normally, other scholars use the Sutra **स्वस्थे वारा** or **स्वस्थे दाराह** and say that the Dasa of a sign whose lord is placed in the sign itself is of 12 years duration. However, as per our author, we need to count from the Dasa sign to the sign occupied by a planet immediately behind it. In the present case, as the Dasa duration is being calculated used zodiacal and reverse order for odd and even signs respectively, we have to count from Pisces, the Dwadasamsa sign of Saturn, to Taurus, the sign occupied by a planet immediately behind Pisces, following the anti-zodiacal reckoning. This gives the duration of Saturn Dasa as 11 years.

ततश्चन्द्रानंतरभागकलस्य रवेः पञ्च | ततश्शुक्रस्य दश | एवं दशाक्रमः | पाचकास्तु शन्यादयश्शुक्रान्तास्तत्रकल्पिताद्वादशग्रहाएव | नतु द्वादश..(राश)यः |

The Dasa of next planet Sun is of 5 years and finally, Venus Dasa gets a span of 10 years. This is the sequence of Dasas. The *Pachakas* for the Dasas will be Saturn and other 12 planets respectively placed in the Svamsa Chakra and not the 12 signs.

NOTES: The next Dasa of Sun placed in Cancer in Svamsa Chakra will be of 5 years as he attains the Dwadasamsa of Virgo. The longitude of the Sun is given as 2. 07°.47'. Ignoring the sign, when the degrees and minutes of the Sun are applied to Cancer, the Dwadasamsa will be of the 4th sign Libra. However, as per this discussion the Sun should have gained three Dwadasamsas only there by attaining Virgo. Hence, I suspect a corruption in the manuscript here and the longitude of the Sun could be 2.07°.27' in the place of the one provided. The last Dasa of Venus placed in Leo in Svamsa is of 10 years duration as Venus attains the Dwadasamsa of Libra.

This is a planetary Dasa based on the Svamsa Chakra. The author has not mentioned the name of this Dasa. I would like to refer it as **Svamsa Chakra Karaka Dasa** until a proper name of this Dasa comes to the fore from other manuscripts or treatises. This is the second Dasa explained by our author after the Drik Dasa. The method of interpreting the Dasa results will be presented in the next paragraphs.

The readers are requested to note that the author is not using the so-called Varga Chakras of modern age. Planetary aspects, conjunctions, Dasa years and so on are considered from the Rasi Chakra only.

अस्मिन्चक्रे फलयोजना | कन्यांशगत अधिकभागगतआत्मा | फलंतद्दशायां पञ्चमेवर्षे मृत्युवज्जायाग्नि कणश्च ||१|२|७|| अग्निकृतं व्रणं चिह्नम् |

The method of predicting results from this Chakra will be explained now. The Atma who has attained greatest degrees is placed in Virgo. In this Dasa, during the 5th year of the native following the Sutra **मृत्युवज्जायाग्नि कणश्च** ||१|२|७||, the native will suffer burning from fire and will develop a wound mark caused by burning.

NOTES: From this we can infer that the results attributed to the presence of the Atma Karaka in the 12 signs in Svamsa can be applied during the first Dasa or subsequent Dasas of the Atma Karaka. The time of fructification of the results can be at the end of the Dasa.

कन्यायामेव अंश...बन्धात्पितृ राजमूलाद्बहुधनलाभः | किं च | कन्यापेक्षया धनाधिपशुक्रस्य तल्लाभे कर्कटे स्फुटगत्यास्थितत्वेन तत्रलाभकारकतया रवेः कल्पनात् | धनाधिपे लाभ..(गते लाभेशे) धनमागते | तावुभौकेन्द्रगौवापि धनलाभमुदीरयेत् | इति धनलाभश्च | पितुर्धनलाभो भवति |

From this sign Virgo itself, as there is a connection…with Amsa, the native's father will gain wealth because of the ruler. The reason for such result is explained now. Venus, the 2nd lord from Virgo is placed in the 11th in Cancer in the Rasi Chakra while in the Svamsa Chakra, the Sun is placed in Cancer in the 11th. As per the rule – when the 11th lord is placed in the 2nd or the 2nd lord is placed in the 11th or when both the 11th and 2nd lords are placed in Kendras, gain of wealth is to be predicted – the native's father experiences this favourable result of gaining wealth.

NOTES: The Svamsa sign occupied by the Dasa lord is to be considered as the Lagna and the relative position of planets in the Rasi Chakra and the Svamsa Chakra from that sign are to be blended to give the interpretation. In this case, Venus, the 2nd lord from the Svamsa sign Virgo, is placed in Cancer in Rasi Chakra that happens to be the 11th from Virgo. In the Svamsa Chakra, the Sun is placed in Cancer. Thus, blending the influence of the Sun, Venus, 2nd and 11th houses it is interpreted that the native's father will gain wealth during this Dasa.

पञ्चवर्षादूर्ध्वं कुजस्य एकादशवर्षादशा | अंशेतु शुभचक्रसंबन्धा.......लाभाधिक्यमस्ति | राहुकेतुभ्यां तृतीय(लाभ)पञ्चमाभ्यां दृष्टत्वात् | पितृभ्रातृक्लेशोभवति | आहत्यषोडश |

After the native completes his 5th year, the next Dasa of Mars will be for 11 years. As it is a benefic sign in the (Sv)amsa, the native will experience gains. As the 11th and 5th signs have the association and aspect of Rahu and Ketu, the native's brothers and father will face difficulties. The total years by the end of Mars Dasa will be 16.

NOTES: The benefic and malefic nature of the Svamsa sign occupied by the Dasa lord will have a prominent influence on the favourable and unfavourable nature of the results experienced by the native. Here, Mars occupies Libra in Svamsa Chakra and hence benefic results like gain of wealth are interpreted. With reference to Libra, the 5th sign Aquarius and the 11th sign Leo in the Rasi Chakra are occupied by the nodes. This indicates hard time for the native's brothers and father. The original reads as *Triteeyapanchamaabhyaam Drustatvaat* which means Rahu and Ketu should aspect the 3rd and 5th. When reckoned from the Svamsa sign Libra, there is no aspect of Rahu and Ketu on the 3rd sign Sagittarius. If the Janma Lagna Leo is considered, there is no aspect of Rahu and Ketu on the 5th sign Sagittarius. Hence, I suspect a corruption in the manuscript here.

तदूर्ध्वं राहुदशा द्वादशवर्षा | मिथुनेराहुद्वादशांशे पापसंबन्धात् सर्वस्वहानिः | स्वजनारिष्टं च भवति | तदुक्तं | यस्मिन्नंशेक्रूरस्तस्यदशायां करोतिवैकल्यम् | पापद्वयसंबन्धेमरणं तत्रार्थनाशोऽपि || इति |
This is followed by the Dasa of Rahu of 12 years. As the Dwadasamsa sign of Rahu, Gemini, is associated with malefic planets, there will be all-round destruction (of wealth). The native's kith and kin will face death and dangers. It is said – Dasa of a planet which has malefic association in its Amsa (Dwadasamsa) will cause unfortunate incidents. When there is association of two malefic planets there will be death and loss of wealth.

NOTES: The next Dasa of Rahu is said to cause severe calamities to the native. The reason attributed is the presence of malefic planets Sun and Mars in Gemini which happens to be the Dwadasamsa of Rahu who is placed in Scorpio in the Svamsa Chakra. We can thus infer another rule of interpretation here. If the Dwadasamsa sign of the Dasa lord is associated with two or more malefic planets in the Rasi Chakra, death and destruction is to be predicted during the Dasa.

ततोधनुश्शनिदशा पञ्चवर्षा । तस्य जात.....त्वाद्राजयोगप्रदत्वम् ।

The next Dasa of Saturn placed in Sagittarius will be of 5 years. There, because of….the native will enjoy Raja Yoga.

NOTES: The manuscript has a gap here where the author explains the reasons for the Raja Yoga. With the understanding of the Upajeevya Raja Yogas explained elsewhere in the text, I would try to explain this portion. The Bhagakaladhika Atma Karaka Saturn is placed in Sagittarius in the Rasi Chakra. In the Svamsa Chakra also, the Atma Karaka Saturn is placed in the same sign Sagittarius which happens to be the 5th house from the Janma Lagna Leo. Thus, a sort of Upajeevya Yoga is formed by the Atma Karaka's position in the Rasi Chakra and his position in the Svamsa Chakra thereby generating a Raja Yoga. Hence, the native will experience very good developments in life during the 5 years of Saturn Dasa in Sagittarius Svamsa.

केतुदशा चतुर्वर्षा । तस्यापीश्वरसंबन्धात्तत्रापिधनदत्वम् । आहत्य सप्तत्रिंशत् ।

The Dasa of Ketu will be of 4 years. As it has the association of the lord (Atma Karaka as per the Sutra *Sa Eeshte*), this Dasa also proves to be prosperous. The cumulative age of the native by the end of Ketu Dasa would be 37 years.

NOTES: The next Dasa of Ketu placed in Capricorn Svamsa is also said to cause wealth and prosperity because of the association with *Eeshwara*, the Atma Karaka. As per the definition of the Upajeevyatva, Ketu in Capricorn in the Svamsa Chakra is placed immediately next to the sign occupied by the Atma Karaka in the Rasi and Svamsa Chakras. From this, another rule of interpretation can be deduced. If the Svamsa Dasa planet, by being placed in the same sign in the Svamsa Chakra, has Upajeevya Yoga with the Atma Karaka or Amatya Karaka posited in the 5th or 9th signs from the Janma Lagna in the Rasi Chakra, there will be Raja Yoga. If the Svamsa Dasa planet has Upajeevya Yogas with the Karakas by being placed in the immediately adjacent signs, then a mere Dhana Yoga will form.

तदुपरि गुरुमहादशा पञ्चवर्षा । अत्रमहान्क्लेशः । अर्थभेदः । समा....ष्ठम् । रोगप्राबल्यं च भवति ।

The next Dasa of Jupiter is of 5 years duration. Here, the native will experience great difficulties and loss of wealth. There will be death and dangers to the native's kith and kin. There will be great suffering because of diseases.

NOTES: The Dasa of Jupiter who is placed in Aquarius in the Svamsa Chakra is said to cause such bad results. The reasons could be: (i) The Dasa of Jupiter is the 6th in sequence and hence can cause such difficulties including illness. It seems that the 6th, 8th and 12th Dasas in the sequence would be generally unfavourable in nature. (ii) Aquarius is a malefic sign and it is occupied by debilitated Ketu in the Rasi Chakra.

ततो मीन(शनि)दशाचतुर्वर्षा | अत्रत्य? शनेरनीश्वरत्वात् पापमात्रत्वेन कष्टफलं | अत्र पूर्ववचनम् | अशुभमवश्यंवाच्यं दशावसानेषुसर्वत्र | नीचारिराशिगानां पापा.....षेणेति ||

The Dasa of Saturn placed in Pisces is of 4 years. Here, as the *Eeshwaratva* of Saturn does not apply in this sign and only his malefic nature will be expressed, the native faces difficulties. Here, as per the saying **अशुभमवश्यंवाच्यं दशावसानेषु सर्वत्र**, at the end of every Dasa, difficulties and unfortunate events should be predicted to the native.

NOTES: In the case of Saturn Dasa placed in Pisces Svamsa, Saturn does not form any Upajeevyatva connection and hence he will behave as a natural malefic planet thereby causing difficulties to the native. Further, his Dwadasamsa sign Sagittarius is occupied by malefic Saturn in the Rasi Chakra. A general rule can be inferred here from the saying **अशुभमवश्यंवाच्यं दशावसानेषु सर्वत्र** that the junction between any two Dasas would generally cause unfavourable results.

ततोबुधदशा षड्वर्षा | अत्र किंचित्सौख्यं | वृश्चिके उच्चरा(हु)ग्निकल्पनात् द्वितीये उच्चचन्द्रकल्पनाच्च बहुशुभत्वकारकत्वेऽपि अष्टमदशा किंचित्सौख्यमित्युक्तम् | आहत्य (द्वि)पञ्चाशत् |

After that, the 6 years Dasa of Mercury will give minor comforts to the native. Though the placement of exalted Rahu in Scorpio and exalted Moon in the 2nd in the Svamsa Chakra should indicate great fortune to the native, only little comforts are predicted as this Mercury Dasa happens to be the 8th Dasa. The total years by the end of Mercury Dasa are 52.

NOTES: Here, we can see that the planetary position in the Svamsa Chakra has been considered with reference to the Svamsa sign of the Dasa lord. It can be understood that the presence of exalted planets in the 8th and 2nd signs from the Dasa lord would bless the native with immense fortune during the Dasa. However, as the Dasa of Mercury happens to be the 8th in the sequence, it is said that the native would experience only little comforts. Hence, it can be inferred that the Dasa being 6th or 8th or 12th in the sequence will nullify even the powerful good Yogas and make the native experience ordinary comforts only.

तदुपरि चन्द्रदशा पञ्चवर्षा....| (उ)च्चत्वाद्धनलाभाधिकमस्ति | समानजनक्लेशश्च | तच्च स्वल्पं | द्वितीये मिथुने शनेः कल्पनात् स्वभावावस्थायां च पापद्वयसंबन्धात् |

The next Dasa of the Moon is of 5 years…..here, as the Moon is exalted, gain of wealth can be predicted. However, there will be death and danger to the native's kith and kin. But, the troubles will be less intense. The minor unfortunate events are predicted because of the placement of Saturn in the 2nd in Gemini and also the sign getting associated with two malefic planets in the Rasi Chakra.

NOTES: The Dasa of a planet who occupies exaltation sign in Svamsa Chakra would cause benefic results like gain of wealth and so on. This is further confirmed because of the presence of the 2nd lord Mercury in Taurus in the Rasi Chakra while the Dasa lord Moon is placed in the 11th joining the 11th lord Jupiter. However, problems to the kith and kin of the native are predicted here because, the 2nd sign Gemini is occupied by malefic Saturn in the Svamsa Chakra and two malefic planets - the Sun and Mars - in the Rasi Chakra. The 2nd sign rules over the native's family which, thus affected by malefic planets, can cause such unfortunate results to the family members. The unfortunate events would be less in severity because of the general strength of the Dasa lord Moon.

तदुपरि मिथुनशनिदशा एकादशवर्षा | मीने शुभद्वयसंबन्धा.......शुभकालः | तदुक्तं | तुङ्गग्रहेणापि शुभेनदृष्टः करोति युक्तोऽपि नरं महीशमिति || आहत्य सप्तपञ्चाशदुपरि अष्टषष्टिपर्यन्तं उत्तरोत्तरं शुभकालः |

The next Dasa of Saturn placed in Gemini is of 11 years. As two benefic planets are associated with Pisces….this period will be auspicious. Because it is said, if the sign is occupied or aspected by an exalted planet or a benefic planet, the native will become a king. Hence, starting from the 57th year to the 68th year of the native, the period will be progressively auspicious and fortunate.

NOTES: The Dwadasamsa sign of the Dasa lord Saturn who is placed in Gemini in Svamsa Chakra is Pisces. This is occupied by two benefic planets – the Moon and Jupiter – in the Rasi Chakra. Hence, the Dasa would cause favourable results to the native. Note that the sign Gemini itself is afflicted by two malefic planets, the Sun and Mars, in the Rasi Chakra. However, it seems that this negative impact is overridden by the benefic influence of the Dwadasamsa sign Pisces.

तदुपरि कर्कटरविदशा पञ्चवर्षा | अत्रक्ले(शकाल:?)........|

The next Dasa of the Sun placed in Cancer will be of 5 years. In this period the native will face difficulties(?)…..

NOTES: Because of the missing portion in the manuscript the result of Sun Dasa is not clear. However, there is a hint for unfavourable results. This could be possible because the 2nd, 8th and 12th signs from Cancer are occupied by malefic planets in the Rasi Chakra.

आत्मनो भावपांशस्य चोत्तमादि च पूर्ववत् | भावपांशदशाज्ञेया भावेशालोकभे मृतिः || अस्यार्थः | आत्मनः अधिकभागकलस्य योराशिस्तस्य च तदपेक्षया अष्टमाधिपतिर्यस्मिन् राशौ वर्तते | त....द्वादशांशः | तस्य च पूर्ववत् उत्तमादिज्ञेयम् |

The meaning of the Shloka **आत्मनो भावपांशस्य चोत्तमादिच पूर्ववत् | भावपांशदशाज्ञेया भावेशालोकभे मृतिः ||** is, considering the nature of the sign occupied by the Atma (Bhagakaladhika Karaka) and the nature of the Dwadasamsa sign occupied by the lord of the 8th house from the Atma, the longevity of the native is to be decided as explained before.

NOTES: The author suddenly takes up the matter of Atmano Bhavapamsa Dasa here while discussing the Dasa of the Sun who is placed in Cancer in Svamsa Chakra. This might be to remind us that Cancer happens to be the Dwadasamsa sign of the Moon, the 8th lord from the sign occupied by the Bhagakaladhika Atma Karaka Saturn in Rasi Chakra. This might also be the reason for attributing unfortunate results to this Sun Dasa. This is the third Dasa mentioned by our author.

In the Atmano Bhavapamsa Dasa, normally the nature of the sign occupied by the Atma Karaka and the nature of the Navamsa sign occupied by the 8th lord from the Lagna are considered by other authorities following Prakruti Chakra and Pada Krama reckoning. Readers may refer to the book Jataka Sara Sangraha translated by me for further information. Our author considers the 8th lord of the sign occupied by the Atma Karaka instead of the 8th lord from the Lagna. Further, instead of the Navamsa sign occupied by the 8th lord, the Dwadasamsa sign is considered.

तत्प्रकारस्तु । चरेचरस्थिरद्वंद्वाः स्थिरेद्वंद्वचरस्थिराः । द्वंद्वे स्थिरोभयचरा द्विवा(जीव)रोगमृतिः क्रमात् ॥ अत्रद्वि(जी)वेति दीर्घमायुः । रोगइतिमध्यमायुः । मृत्युरित्यल्पायुः ।

The method of longevity determination based on the nature of the signs will be explained now. For a movable sign the movable, fixed and dual signs; for a fixed sign the dual, movable and fixed signs; for a dual sign the fixed, dual and movable signs respectively form the *Jiva*, *Roga* and *Mruti*. Here, *Jiva* means long span of life, *Roga* means medium span of life, and *Mrutyu* means short span of life.

NOTES: Let us take the present horoscope as an example. The Bhagakaladhika Atma Karaka Saturn occupies Sagittarius in the Rasi Chakra which is a dual sign. The 8th lord from Saturn is the Moon. The Moon who is placed in Pisces in Rasi Chakra attains the Dwadasamsa of Cancer which is a movable sign. Thus, the pair of signs turns out to be dual and movable which should indicate short life span for the native. However, the native seems to have lived up to a long-span of life. Nevertheless, there are many exceptional rules to be applied to this Dasa which were not mentioned by our author or which were missed by us because of the corruption in the manuscript.

एवं प्रकारेण पूर्वशास्त्रोक्तप्रकारेण आयुर्ज्ञात्वा दशाः कल्पयेत् । आत्मनः अष्टमाधिपतिस्थितराशिद्वादशांशराशिमारभ्य दशासुनीतासु तदालोकनराशिदशायां मृतिः ।

In this way, after the life span of the native is determined following the injunctions of the previous treatises, Dasas are to be prepared. Starting the Dasas from the Dwadasamsa sign occupied by the 8th lord from the Atma Karaka, the native's death is to be predicted in the Dasa of the sign aspected by the 8th lord.

NOTES: In the present horoscope, the Atmano Bhavapamsa Dasa is to be taken from Cancer, the Dwadasamsa sign occupied by the Moon, the 8th lord from the Atma Karaka Saturn. The native's death is to be predicted during the Dasa of a sign aspected by the 8th lord Moon, i.e. during one of the Dasas of Gemini, Virgo and Sagittarius.

आहत्य त्रिसप्ततिः |७३| तदुपरि शुक्रदशा दशवर्षा | परमायुस्त्र्यशीतिः |

By the end of the Sun Dasa, the native would complete his 73 years. The next Dasa is of Venus having 10 years duration. The maximum longevity of the native by this Dasa is 83 years.

NOTES: Now, we are back to the Svamsa Chakra Karaka Dasa. By the end of the Dasa of Sun placed in Cancer in the Svamsa Chakra, the native would complete 73 years of age. Adding 10 years of the next and last Dasa of Venus the maximum longevity of the native turns out to be 83 years.

प्राकारस्तु | अधिकभागकल आत्मा स्फुटवशाद्यत्रस्थितः तदारभ्यैव | नतु द्वादशांशराशिमारभ्य | तदादि ग्रहकल्पनमात्रम् | एवं कल्पित ग्रहे ......अधिकभागकलमात्मानं लग्नभावंमत्वा तदादि द्वादशभावान् ज्ञात्वा तत्तद्ग्रहैः कल्पितग्रहैः | तत्ररवौराजकार्यपरः ||१|२|१४|| इत्यादिफलं योजनीयम् | तत्रकल्पितानां द्वादशांशद्वारा (शुभा)शुभविचारः |

The method is explained now. The sign occupied by the *Bhagakaladhika Atma Karaka* in the Rasi Chakra is to be considered as the starting point (Lagna). His Dwadasamsa position should not be considered for reckoning the 12 Bhavas. That position is only to be used to place other planets in the Svamsa Chakra. In this way, considering the sign occupied by the Atma Karaka in the Rasi Chakra as Lagna in the Svamsa Chakra, the position of planets in the Svamsa in the 12 bhavas should be considered to judge the results of the Sutras like तत्ररवौराजकार्यपरः ||१|२|१४||. Considering the *Dwadasamsa* of the planets placed in the *Svamsa Chakra*, the favourable and unfavourable results are to be interpreted.

NOTES: There appears to be a gap here in the manuscript as the text starts abruptly with the words 'the method is explained now'. However, from the context we can infer that the method to interpret the results of the Svamsa Chakra is being explained. Here, we are asked to consider the actual position of the Bhagakaladhika Atma Karaka in the Rasi Chakra as the reference point or Lagna in the Svamsa Chakra and to judge the twelve bhavas based on the nature of planets placed in them in the Svamsa Chakra and applying the Sutras mentioned for the Svamsa Chakra in the 2nd quarter of the 1st chapter of the Jaimini Sutras starting with the Sutra **अथ स्वांशो ग्रहाणां.**

The Dwadasamsa signs of the planets in the Svamsa Chakra as considered for the Svamsa Chakra Karaka Dasa are to be applied to know the good and bad results. This means, ignoring the sign occupied by the planets in the Rasi Chakra and considering their degrees and minutes in the signs they occupy in the Svamsa Chakra, their respective Dwadasamsa signs are to be determined. If the Dwadasamsa signs are occupied by malefic planets in the Rasi Chakra malefic results are to be predicted. Contrarily, if the Dwadasamsa signs are occupied by benefic planets in the Rasi Chakra, favourable results are to be predicted.

य.....दि ग्रहैः फलमुच्यते । तत्र तत्र स्वांशचक्रग्रहेणसह स्फुटग्रहंवा ~~चक्रग्रहंवा~~ ग्रहचक्रग्रहंवा संयोज्य फलंवाच्यम् । पूर्णेन्दुशुक्रयोः भोगीविद्याजीवीच ॥१।२।१५॥ तत्रमन्दसर्पयोः ताम्बूलदायी ॥१।२।२३॥ इत्यादि स......(पदचक्रे)तु पूर्वचक्रद्वयग्रहचक्रवशात् स्फुटग्रहवशाच्च द्वित्र्यादिग्रहफलं योजनीयम् ।

...considering the planets, results are to be predicted. Blending the position of planets in the respective signs in the Svamsa Chakra with that of Rasi Chakra or Graha Chakra the results of Sutras like **पूर्णेन्दुशुक्रयोः भोगीविद्याजीवीच ॥१।२।१५॥ तत्रमन्दसर्पयोः ताम्बूलदायी ॥१।२।२३॥** are to be interpreted. In the case of Pada Chakra, considering the planetary positions in the first two Chakras (Svamsa Chakra and Pada Chakra) and Graha Chakra along with the Rasi Chakra positions, the combined influence of two or three or more planets is to be interpreted.

उपपदाधिकारे तु पूर्वचक्रत्रयग्रहैः स्फुटग्रहेणसह द्वित्र्यादिग्रहफलंचिन्तनीयम् । एवमुत्तरोत्तरादि ......र्व पूर्वाधिकार सापेक्षत्वम् । तत्तदधिकारोपदेशादेव ज्ञायते । तत्रापि स्वांशपदयोरन्योन्य नित्यप्राप्तैक्षिसापेक्षत्वमुभयत्रादेशवशात् ज्ञायते । एवमत्रशास्त्रे प्रक्रिया ।

In the case of Upapada Adhikara (the section of Jaimini Sutras mentioned in the 4th quarter of the 1st chapter dealing with the interpretation of Upapada), the planetary position in the first three

Chakras (Svamsa Chakra, Pada Chakra, and Upapada Chakra) along with their positions in the Rasi Chakra are to be overlaid in each sign and the combined influence of two or three or more planets is to be predicted. Thus, the results mentioned in the previous sections of the Jaimini Sutras are to be applied to the subsequent sections. Here also, the fact that the Svamsa and Pada are mutually interdependent on each other will become clear when we see that the results attributed to each of them in their respective sections are asked to apply to both of them. This is the methodology to be followed in this science.

NOTES: Our author explains here a method of applying various rules mentioned in the respective sections of Svamsa, Pada and Upapada Adhikaranas in the 2nd, 3rd and 4th quarters of the 1st chapter of the Jaimini Sutras. In the case of Svamsa Chakra, the planetary positions in a sign in the Svamsa Chakra, Rasi Chakra and Graha Chakra are to be blended to apply the results mentioned in the 2nd quarter. In the case of Pada Chakra, the planetary positions in the Svamsa Chakra, Pada Chakra, Rasi Chakra and Graha Chakra are to be blended to interpret the results mentioned in the 3rd quarter. In the case of Upapada Chakra, the planetary positions in the Svamsa Chakra, Pada Chakra and Upapada Chakra are to be considered along with those of the Rasi Chakra to apply the results mentioned in the 4th quarter. Note that the Graha Chakra is excluded for the Upapada Chakra. The author further says that the rules mentioned in the previous sections will become applied to the subsequent sections. It means that the Sutras of the 2nd quarter are to be applied for interpreting Svamsa Chakra results. The Sutras of the 2nd and 3rd quarters are to be applied to the Pada Chakra. Finally, the Sutras of the 2nd, 3rd and 4th quarters are to be applied to the Upapada Chakra. The author also says that the results of the Sutras dealing with Svamsa Chakra and Pada Chakra can be applied to both of them. Thus, the Sutras of 2nd and 3rd quarters can be applied to both Svamsa Chakra and Pada Chakra.

प्रकृते ....भागकलाक्रांतत्वाद्धनुर्लग्नम् | तदा वृश्चिकांता द्वादशभावाः | पदचक्रे तु | लग्नाधिपतिना प्रागवस्थितराशिमारभ्य द्वादशभावाः | रविचक्रे तु रविंध्रुवंकृत्वा तदादि द्वादशभावाः | एवं चतुर्विधचक्रक्रमः | प्रथमं स्वांशचक्रं प्रदर्शितम् | इतरचक्रत्रयं क्रमेणप्रदर्शइष्यामः |

In the present case, the *Bhagakaladhika Karaka* Saturn occupies Sagittarius. Hence, Sagittarius is to be considered as the Lagna and the 12 Bhavas ending with Scorpio should be studied in the Svamsa Chakra. In the case of *Pada Chakra*, the first sign occupied by the Lagna lord is to be considered as the Lagna. In the *Ravi Chakra* (Graha Chakra), the position of the Sun in the Rasi Chakra is to be fixed and the 12 houses are to be studied with reference to the Sun. In this way the Bhavas are to be analysed in the four Chakras. The first of them, Svamsa Chakra, has been demonstrated earlier. The remaining three Chakras will be explained sequentially in the following lines.

तत्रादौ पदचक्रम् | प्रकृतजातके लग्नं सिंहः | रविर्मिथुने | ततश्च | यावदीशाश्रयम् ||१|१|२७|| इति मेषं पदम् | तत्र रविः तत्केन्द्रेषु कल्पयेत् | मेषादि केन्द्रान्तरालेषु चतसृषु रव्यादिग्रहान् स्थितिक्रमेण द्वौद्वौ कल्पयेत् | तथाहि | मेषे रविः | वृषभे कुजः | मिथुने शुक्रः | कर्कटके रविः | सिंहे राहुः | कन्यायां शनिः | तुलायां रविः | वृश्चिके केतुः | धनुषि चन्द्रः | मकरे रविः | कुंभे गुरुः | मीने बुधः | एवं द्वादशकल्पना | ~~कर्कटके रविः~~ | व्यये सग्रहे ग्रहदृष्टेवा श्रीमन्तः ||१|३|२|| इत्यादिफलमस्मिन्चक्रे योजनीयम् |

Merc	PADAM Sun	Mars	Ven
Jup	PADA CHAKRAM		Sun
Sun			Rahu
Moon	Ketu	Sun	Sat

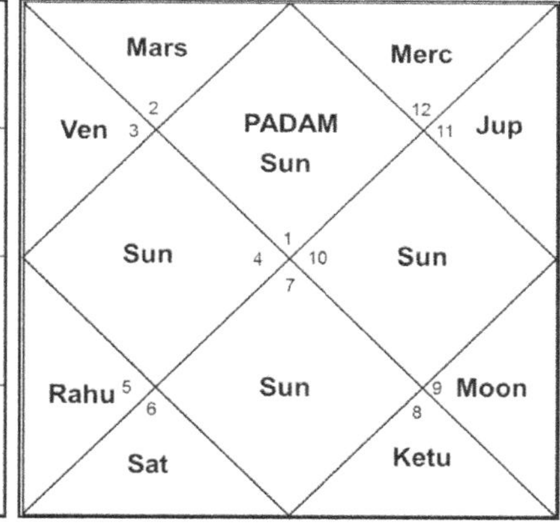

First the Pada Chakra will be taken up. In the present horoscope the Lagna is Leo. Its lord Sun is placed in the 11th in Gemini. Following the Sutra **यावदीशाश्रयं** ||१|१|२७||, the 11th sign from Gemini, Aries, will be the Pada. In the Pada Chakra, the Lagna lord Sun is thus placed in the Pada in Aries and in its Kendras. The remaining eight planets in the sequential order of their position in the Rasi Chakra with respect to the Lagna lord Sun are to be placed in the intervening two-two signs between the four Kendras from the Pada Aries. Thus, the

Pada Chakra for this horoscope will have the planets in this order – the Sun in Aries in the Pada, Mars in Taurus, Venus in Gemini, the Sun in Cancer, Rahu in Leo, Saturn in Virgo, the Sun in Libra, Ketu in Scorpio, the Moon in Sagittarius, the Sun in Capricorn, Jupiter in Aquarius, and Mercury in Pisces. In this way the twelve signs in the Pada Chakra are to be filled up with the nine planets. The results of the Sutras like व्यये सग्रहे ग्रहदृष्टेवा श्रीमन्तः ||१|३|२|| mentioned in the 3rd quarter of the 1st chapter of Jaimini Sutras are to be applied to this Chakra.

NOTES: The author asks us to apply the Sutras mentioned in the 3rd quarter to this Chakra and interpret those results. However, there are some questions that arise at this point. For example, the Sutra व्यये सग्रहे ग्रहदृष्टेवा श्रीमन्तः means that, when the 11th house from the Pada is occupied or aspected by a planet, the native will be wealthy. Normally, this rule is applied to the Rasi Chakra and prosperity is predicted for the native. However, we are asked to apply this rule to the Pada Chakra where for every horoscope the 11th sign from the Pada will have a planet receiving aspects from three other planets. The same problem arises while applying other Sutras also.

उपपदं तु सप्तमं कुंभम् | शनिर्धनुषि | उपपदं पदं पित्र्यनुचरात् ||१|४|१|| इत्युपपदं तुला | तत्र शनिः | तत्केन्द्रेषु शनिं कल्पयेत् | तुलादि केन्द्रान्तरालेषु चतसृषु प्राग्वच्छन्यादिग्रहान् द्वौद्वौ ग्रहस्थितिक्रमेण कल्पयेत् | तथा हि | तुलायां शनिः | वृश्चिके केतुः | धनुषिचन्द्रः | मकरे शनिः | कुंभे गुरुः | मीने बुधः | मेषे शनिः | वृषभे रविः | मिथुने कुजः | कर्कटके शनिः | सिंहे शुक्रः | कन्यायां राहुः | एवं ग्रहकल्पना | तुलादिकन्यान्तं द्वादशभावाः ||

Merc	Sat	Sun	Mars
Jup	UPAPADA CHAKRAM		Sat
Sat			Ven
Moon	Ketu	UPAPADAM Sat	Rahu

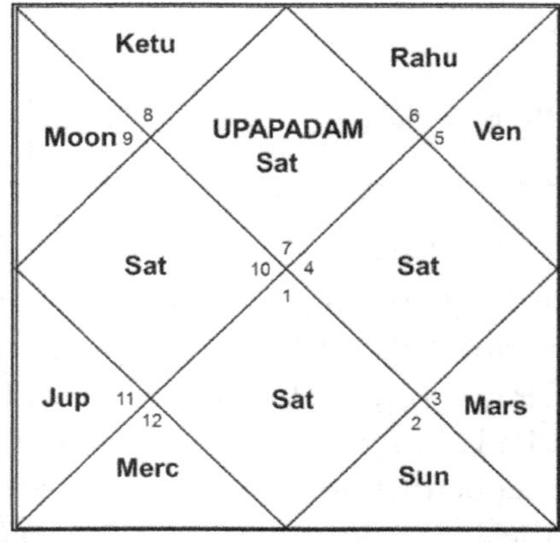

Now, the Upapada Chakra for this horoscope will be explained. Here, the 7th house is Aquarius whose lord Saturn is placed in Sagittarius. Following the Sutra उपपदं पदं पित्र्यनुचरात् ||१|४|१||, Upapada will fall in Libra. Hence, in the Upapada Chakra, the 7th lord Saturn is to be placed in Libra and its Kendra signs. The remaining eight planets in the sequential order of their position in the Rasi Chakra with respect to the 7th lord Saturn are to be placed in the intervening two-two signs between the four Kendras from the Upapada Libra as done before for the Pada Chakra. Thus, the Upapada Chakra for this horoscope will have the planets in this order –Saturn in the Upapada in Libra, Ketu in Scorpio, the Moon in Sagittarius, Saturn in Capricorn, Jupiter in Aquarius, Mercury in Pisces, Saturn in Aries, the Sun in Taurus, Mars in Gemini, Saturn in Cancer, Venus in Leo and Rahu in Virgo. Thus the planets are to be placed in the 12 signs of the Upapada Chakra and the 12 houses are to be reckoned starting from Upapada Libra and ending with its 12th sign Virgo.

Jup	Sat	Merc	Sun
Moon	GRAHA CHAKRAM		Mars
Ketu			Ven
Ven	Sat	Jup	Rahu

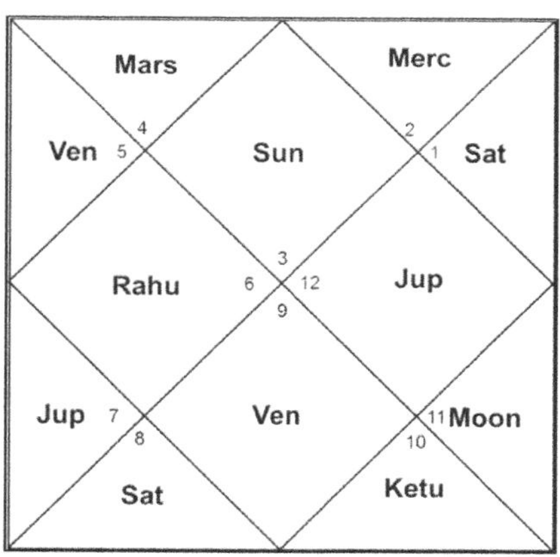

ग्रह......|| रविर्मिथुने ध्रुवंविदित्वा तदादि ग्रहस्थितिक्रमेण पूर्वार्धपरार्धयोरंतरांतरान् कल्पयेत् | शिष्टेषु त्रिषु भावेषु चक्रमप्राप्तोग्रहे........| तथा हि | मिथुने रविः | कर्कटके कुजः | सिंहे शुक्रः | कन्यायां राहुः | तुलायां गुरुः | वृश्चिके शनिः | धनुषि शुक्रः | मकरे केतुः | कुंभे चन्द्रः | मीने गुरुः | मेषे शनिः | वृषभे बुधः | एवं द्वादशभावकल्पनाक्रमः |

Now, the Graha Chakra for this horoscope will be explained. Fixing the Sun in Gemini, the sign occupied by him in the Rasi Chakra, the remaining planets with reference to the Sun are to be placed in the Graha Chakra in the sequential order of their position in the Rasi Chakra, leaving intervening gaps in the first half and second half of the zodiac. In the remaining three empty signs of the Graha Chakra...... Thus, the Graha Chakra for this horoscope will have the planets in this order – the Sun in Gemini, Mars in Cancer, Venus in Leo, Rahu in Virgo, Jupiter in Libra, Saturn in Scorpio, Venus in Sagittarius, Ketu in Capricorn, the Moon in Aquarius, Jupiter in Pisces, Saturn in Aries, and Mercury in Taurus. In this way, the 12 Bhavas are also to be considered starting from Gemini, the sign occupied by the Sun in the Rasi Chakra.

NOTES: The text is difficult to understand here because of the gaps in the manuscript. However, after studying the planetary positions mentioned in the Graha Chakra we can understand the intention of the author. I am thankful to my dear friend Shanmukha for helping me to decipher this aspect of the manuscript. After fixing the position of the Sun in Gemini, the 2nd, 3rd, 4th and 6th signs are to be filled with the planets Mars, Venus, Rahu and Saturn respectively as per their sequential position from the Sun in the Rasi Chakra. Note that the 5th sign has been left empty. Next, leaving the 7th sign Sagittarius empty, the 8th, 9th, 10th and 12th signs are to be filled with the remaining planets Ketu, Moon, Jupiter and Mercury respectively. Note that the 11th sign is left empty here. When counted from the 7th house Sagittarius these signs will be 2nd, 3rd, 4th and 6th signs occupied by planets while the 5th sign (11th from the Sun) is empty. Thus, with reference to the Sun, the 5th, 7th and 11th signs are left empty while the rest of the signs are filled with the planets as per their sequential order in the Rasi Chakra from the Sun. The 5th sign Libra is to be filled by Jupiter, the Sthira Putra Karaka, the 7th sign Sagittarius is to be filled by Venus, the Sthira Kalatra Karaka, and the 11th sign Aries is to be filled by Saturn, the Sthira Karaka for elder brothers. Thus, the Graha Chakra for this horoscope is prepared. In the case of any other horoscope, the same method is to be followed to prepare the Graha Chakra. Keeping the position of the Sun in the Rasi Chakra fixed, the remaining 8 planets are to be placed in sequential order in the 2nd, 3rd, 4th, 6th, 8th, 9th, 10th and 12th houses from the Sun. The 5th, 7th and 11th houses are to be filled with Jupiter, Venus and Saturn respectively. The process of preparing this Graha Chakra is different from the Graha Chakra mentioned at the Sutra Mando Jyayan Gruheshu at Page No 44.

अस्यच वर्षफलज्ञाने विनियोग.........यनेतु प्रसिद्धग्रहएवग्राह्यः । अत्र संप्रदायः । एकराशौ द्वित्र्यादिग्रहसंभवे प्रसिद्धग्रहचक्रद्वारा वा चक्रगम(न?) कल्पनम् ।

This (Graha Chakra?) is applied in the interpretation of yearly results (Varshaphala or Varshacharya)….in taking up the…..the well-known planet only is to be considered. The traditional practise in this regard is - when two or three or more planets are placed in a sign, the Chakra movement (?) is to be determined based in the well-known Graha Chakra.

NOTES: There appears to be a gap in the manuscript looking at the abruptness of the paragraph. The text here is confusing and I could not come to a conclusion regarding its purport.

शनि(राहु)....कुजकेत्वोश्च एकराशिस्थितौ पूर्वराशौ ग्रहाभावे राहुकेत्वोः प्रातिलोम्यात्पूर्वपूर्वराशौ कल्पना । पूर्वत्र ग्रहेसतिं स्वावस्थित......प्राधम्यमानंतर्यम् । शनिकुजयोस्तस्मिन्नेवराशौ ग्रहांतरसंभवे शनिकुजयोरुत्तरोत्तरराशौ कल्पनमिति ।

If Saturn and Rahu, or Mars and Ketu are placed in the same sign, and there are no planets in the previous sign, Rahu and Ketu are to be placed in the previous signs. When the previous sign is occupied by a planet, the sign occupied by itself…..gains next importance. If Saturn and Mars join other planets in the same sign, then those planets are to be placed in the next signs from Saturn and Mars.

NOTES: This part of the text is also very difficult to comprehend. However, after studying the example horoscope-5, I could make out some sense. When Rahu joins Saturn or Ketu joins Mars, this special rule becomes applicable to calculate the duration of the Dasa years. In such instance, if the previous sign from the sign occupied by Rahu-Saturn or Ketu-Mars is empty then Rahu or Ketu should be placed in the previous sign. If the previous sign is not empty, Rahu or Ketu should be placed in the same sign occupied by them but Saturn or Mars respectively should be placed in the next sign. If the sign lord also joins them, he should be placed in the same sign. If planets other than the sign lord also join Saturn-Rahu or Mars-Ketu, they should be placed in the signs next to Saturn or Mars respectively. Here, I think if more than one planet joins them, they should be placed as per their degree-wise position. This concept will become clear when we discuss the Dasa duration calculated for the example horoscope-5.

दशारंभवर्षचर्यारंभौ तु क्रमेणप्रदर्शइष्यामः । तत्र दशारंभः। प्रथम.....। चन्द्रराशिमारभ्य क्रमेण पञ्चपञ्च घटिकाभिरिष्टकालस्य लग्नमानयेत्। तद्भावलग्नंभवति। तदुक्तम्। कारकक्षांशमारभ्य घटिकानांतु पञ्चकम् । नीत्वा जन्मसमयाद्भावलग्नंप्रचक्षते ॥ ..त्र आत्मकारकश्चन्द्रः । तदाश्रयराशिमंशंवारभ्य भावलग्नकल्पनम्। राशेः कल्पितस्यैव प्राचुर्येण विनियोगः।

The beginning of the Dasa and the Varshacharya will be explained sequentially. First, the beginning of Dasa will be taken up. First (firstly?)….. Starting from the sign occupied by the Moon, arrive at the Lagna by counting one sign for every 5 Ghatis up to the time of birth. This will give the Bhava Lagna. It is said – considering the Amsa or sign of the Karaka as the starting point, count one sign for every 5 Ghatis. The sign arrived up to the time of birth will give the *Bhava Lagna*. Here, the Atma Karaka is the Moon. The sign occupied by the Moon in the Rasi or Amsa is to be considered to calculate the *Bhava Lagna*. However, the Bhava Lagna calculated from the Rasi occupied by the Karaka is widely used in practise.

NOTES: The method of calculating the Bhava Lagna is explained here. As the Moon is referred as the Atma Karaka, I feel that the author refers to another horoscope to explain the method of Bhava Lagna calculation. We need to note one important thing here. Citing the Vruddha Karika **कारकक्षांशमारभ्य घटिकानां तु पञ्चकम्। नीत्वा जन्मसमयाद्भावलग्नं प्रचक्षते ॥**, the author says that there are two methods of calculating the Bhava Lagna – one considering the sign occupied by the Atma Karaka in the Rasi Chakra and the other considering the sign occupied by him in the Amsa. However, he says that the first method is more prevalent in practise. Hence, he considers the Rasi position of the Atma Karaka to calculate the Bhava Lagna. However, it is not clear whether he refers to the Navamsa or Dwadasamsa by the word Amsa.

The method of Bhava Lagna calculation is somewhat different in the available Parasara Hora texts and the readers are requested to note this. We can find the following Sholkas:

सूर्योदयं समारभ्य घटिकानां तु पञ्चकम्। प्रयाति जन्मपर्यन्तं भावलग्नं तदेव हि ॥
इष्टं घट्यादिकं भक्त्वा पञ्चभिर्भाजितं फलम्। यौज्यमौदयिके सूर्ये भावलग्नं स्फुटं च तत्॥

Starting from the sunrise, the Bhava Lagna moves one sign for every five Ghatis from the sign occupied by the Sun, up to the time of native's birth. After dividing the Ishta Kala (birth time in Ghatis and Vighatis) by five, the remainder in degrees and minutes should be added to the longitude of the Sun to derive the exact longitude of the Bhava Lagna. Here, we are asked to consider the sign occupied by the Sun as the basis of the Bhava Lagna while our author asks us to consider the sign occupied by the Bhagakaladhika Karaka as the basis. Further, the method of calculating exact longitude of the Bhava Lagna is not considered. Hence, the position of the Karaka in the every first degree or the very last degree of a sign does not make any difference.

एवं भावलग्नमानीय तत्केन्द्रराशीनां चतुर्णामधिपेषु यस्स्वराश्यपेक्षया अ......स कारकः | तदारभ्य स्थितिक्रमेण सप्तमोऽपि कारकः | तयोर्मध्ये निसर्गबलाधिकः पाचकः | अन्यस्त्वारंभग्रहः | एवं च कारकान् जानीयात् | अवसानग्रहणं आरंभानुरोधेनैव | प्रातिलोम्य......| ...(प्र)थम पाचकमारभ्य नवपाचकान् जानीयात् | भावकेन्द्रपतीनां ग्रहसाम्ये भावलग्नापेक्षया अधिकं गृह्णीयात् |

After calculating the Bhava Lagna in this manner, consider the four Kendras of the Bhava Lagna. Among the lords of these four Kendras, the one who has moved more number of signs when counted from his sign will be the *Karaka*. The seventh planet from such Karaka counted sequentially as per the planetary position in the Rasi Chakra is also a *Karaka*. Between the two Karakas, the planet who is intrinsically strong (Naisargika Bala) is called the *Pachaka*. The other Karaka is called the *Arambhaka*. In this way the Karakas are to be determined. The sequence of the *Pachakas* is to be known following the same sequence of *Arambhakas* and is the *Arambhakas* are in reverse order......starting from the first Pachaka, the nine Pachakas are to be determined. If the lords of the Kendras of Bhava Lagna are equal as per the said criterion, the one who has moved more number of signs with reference to the Bhava Lagna is to be considered.

NOTES: After calculating the Bhava Lagna, the Arambhaka or the starting planet and the Pachaka or the Dasa ruler are to be determined. This will become clear when we study the example horoscope. The nine planets starting from the Arambhaka are to be written down in the order of their sequence in the Rasi Chakra in zodiacal order or the reverse order based on the odd or even nature of the sign occupied by the Arambhaka. Similarly, the nine Pachakas are to be determined starting from the first Pachaka in the same sequence of the Arambhakas. This means, if the sequence of Arambhakas is determined by following zodiacal order, the sequence of Pachakas also follows the zodiacal order. If the sequence of the Arambhakas is determined following anti-zodiacal order, the Pachaka sequence is also to be determined by anti-zodiacal order. Always each Pachaka should be the 7th planet from its respective Arambhaka as per the Rasi Chakra position. The Jaimini Sutra सतल्लाभयोरावर्तते seems to be applied in this concept.

After determining the sequence of Arambhakas and the Pachakas, the duration of the Dasas can be calculated. Counting from the sign occupied by the first Arambhaka to the sign occupied by the first Pachaka in zodiacal or reverse order based on the odd or even nature of the sign occupied by the Arambhaka, the duration of the first Dasa is to be determined. The same procedure is to be applied to determine the duration of the next eight Dasas. The exceptional rules mentioned earlier for the Saturn-Rahu and Mars-Ketu conjunctions are applicable only in the case of Pachaka positions used to calculate the Dasa duration. In the case when these planets are considered as the Arambhakas, their actual position in the Rasi Chakra is to be considered. This is the fourth Dasa dealt by our author and is a planetary Dasa. The author has not mentioned the name of this Dasa. As this Dasa is dependent on the Bhava Lagna, I would like to call this as **Bhava Lagna Karaka Dasa** until another name comes to the fore from other manuscripts or treatises.

प्रकृतजातके तु उक्तरीत्या शनिः | तत्सप्तमकुजश्च | का(रकयोः).....मध्ये कुजो निसर्गबलाधिक इति पाचकः | शनिरारंभकः | तस्य ओजपदगतत्वेन तदापि अनुलोमक्रमेण नवग्रहाज्ञेयाः | पाचकानांतु आरंभानुरोधितया क्रमेण नवग्रहाः ....(ज्ञेयाः)|

In the horoscope under discussion, Saturn will become the Karaka as per the procedure. The 7th planet from Saturn is Mars. Between Saturn and Mars, Mars is intrinsically strong and hence becomes the *Pachaka* while Saturn will become the *Arambhaka*. As the Arambhaka Saturn is placed in an odd (odd-footed?) sign (Sagittarius), the sequence of nine planets is to be counted in zodiacal (normal) order from Saturn. The Pachaka planets are to be counted in the same order used for the Arambhaka planets.

NOTES: In the present horoscope, the Bhagakaladhika Karaka Saturn is to be considered to determine the Bhava Lagna. Saturn is placed in Sagittarius and the native was born 14 Ghatis after Sunrise. Thus counting 5 Ghatis for each sign starting from Sagittarius, the Bhava Lagna will fall in Aquarius. Now, we have to consider the Kendras from the Bhava Lagna and their lords to determine the first Karaka. The Kendras for the Bhava Lagna are Aquarius, Taurus, Leo and Scorpio while their lords are Saturn, Venus, Sun and Mars respectively. When counted from their respective signs, Saturn has moved 11 signs, Venus has moved 3 signs, and the Sun has moved 11 signs while Mars has moved 8 signs. Now, both Saturn and Sun have got equal numbers here. Hence, to determine the Karaka between them, the planet that has moved more number of signs with respect to the Bhava Lagna is to be found. Here, Saturn has moved 11 signs from the Bhava Lagna Aquarius while the Sun has moved 5 signs. Thus, Saturn becomes the first Karaka.

Now, the 7th planet from Saturn as per the positions in the Rasi Chakra will become the second Karaka. In the Rasi Chakra, the planetary sequence with reference to Saturn is – (i) Saturn, (ii) Ketu, (iii) Moon, (iv) Jupiter, (v) Mercury, (vi) Sun, and (vii) Mars. Hence, Mars will become the second Karaka.

Between the two Karakas Saturn and Mars, Mars is stronger as per the Naisargika strength and hence becomes the Pachaka while the other Karaka Saturn becomes the Arambhaka. As the Arambhaka Saturn is placed in an odd sign, the sequence of the Arambhakas is to be determined from Saturn in regular zodiacal order. Thus, the Arambhakas are - (i) Saturn, (ii) Ketu, (iii) Moon, (iv) Jupiter, (v) Mercury, (vi) Sun (vii) Mars, (viii) Venus, and (ix) Rahu. The word used here is *Oja Pada Rasi* which has a different connotation. As per Neelakantha, the signs Aries, Taurus, Gemini, Libra, Scorpio and Sagittarius are odd footed signs while the rest of the signs are even-footed signs. This means, though Taurus and Scorpio are even signs they are treated as odd signs while the signs Leo and Aquarius are treated as even signs despite being odd signs. However, I suspect some corruption here in the manuscript because our author used the normal Prakruti Chakra reckoning in the example horoscopes to count the Dasa years instead of this concept of odd-footed and even-footed signs.

Next, the sequence of the nine Pachakas is to be determined starting from the first Pachaka in the same zodiacal order. Thus, the nine Pachakas are – (i) Mars, (ii) Venus, (iii) Rahu, (iv) Saturn, (v) Ketu, (vi) Moon, (vii) Jupiter, (viii) Mercury, and (ix) the Sun.

तथा च | दशावर्षाणि शन्यादिकुजस्य सप्त | केत्वादिशुक्रस्य षट् | चन्द्रादिराहोर्व्युत्क्रमेणाष्टौ | गुर्वादिशनेर्व्युत्क्रमेण चत्वारि | बुधादिकेतोर्व्युत्क्रमेण चत्वारि | सूर्यादिचन्द्रस्य क्रमेण दश | कुजादि..(गुरोः क्र)मेण दश | शुक्रादिबुधस्यव्युत्क्रमेण त्रीणि | रह्वादिक्रमेणसूर्यस्यैकादश | आहत्य नवग्रहाणां वर्षाणि (त्रि)षष्टिः | तदुपरि पुनरावृत्तौ शन्यादिकुजस्य सप्त | आहत्य सप्त(ति)षष्टिः |

Hence, the Dasa years would be: from Saturn to Mars – 7 years; from Ketu to Venus – 6 years; from the Moon to Rahu in reverse order – 8 years; from Jupiter to Saturn in reverse order – 4 years; from Mercury to Ketu in reverse order – 4 years; from the Sun to the Moon in regular order – 10 years; from Mars to Jupiter in regular order – 10 years; from Venus to Mercury in reverse order – 3 years; from Rahu to the Sun in regular order – 11 years. The total years contributed by the nine planets is 63 years. After that, the Dasa of Saturn to Mars will get repeated which has a duration of 7 years. This totals to a period of 70 years.

Arambhaka	Sign	Pachaka	Sign	Dasa Years
Saturn	Sagittarius	Mars	Gemini	7
Ketu	Aquarius	Venus	Cancer	6
Moon	Pisces	Rahu	Leo	8
Jupiter	Pisces	Saturn	Sagittarius	4
Mercury	Taurus	Ketu	Aquarius	4
Sun	Gemini	Moon	Pisces	10
Mars	Gemini	Jupiter	Pisces	10
Venus	Cancer	Mercury	Taurus	3
Rahu	Leo	Sun	Gemini	11
Saturn	Sagittarius	Mars	Gemini	7

NOTES: Now, the Dasa years are calculated. The first Arambhaka Saturn is in an odd sign Sagittarius. Hence, counting from the first Arambhaka Saturn to the first Pachaka Mars in zodiacal order the duration of the first Dasa will be of 7 years. The second Arambhaka Ketu occupies an odd sign Aquarius. Hence, counting from Ketu to the second Pachaka Venus in zodiacal order, the second Dasa will be of 6 years duration. The third Arambhaka Moon is placed in an even sign Pisces. Therefore, counting from the Moon to the third Pachaka Rahu in anti-zodiacal order, the duration of the third Dasa would be of 8 years. The fourth Arambhaka Jupiter is also placed in an even sign Pisces. Hence, counting from Jupiter to the fourth Pachaka Saturn in anti-zodiacal order, the fourth Dasa would be a period of 4 years. The fifth Arambhaka Mercury is also placed in an even sign Taurus. Thus, counting from Mercury to the fifth Pachaka Ketu in anti-zodiacal order, the fifth Dasa will be of 4 years duration. The sixth Arambhaka Sun is placed in an odd sign Gemini. Hence, counting from the Sun to the sixth Pachaka Moon in zodiacal order, the duration of the sixth Dasa would be of 10 years. The seventh Arambhaka Mars is also placed in Gemini. Thus, counting from Mars to the seventh Pachaka Jupiter, the seventh Dasa would be a period of 10 years. The eighth Arambhaka Venus occupies an even sign Cancer. Therefore, counting from Venus to the eighth Pachaka Mercury in anti-zodiacal order, the eighth Dasa duration will be of 3 years. The ninth and last Arambhaka Rahu is placed in an odd sign Leo. Hence, counting from Rahu to the ninth Pachaka Sun in zodiacal order, the duration of the ninth Dasa is of 11 years. Thus, the total of these nine Dasas would be 63 years (7+6+8+4+4+10+10+3+11). After completion of the first cycle, the Dasas will be repeated again. Thus, the repetition of 7 years of the first Dasa of Saturn and Mars will complete 70 years of the native's age. I would like to draw the attention of the readers to the fact that while calculating the Dasa years, the normal odd nature of Aquarius and Leo and even nature of Taurus and Scorpio are considered instead of their respective Sama Pada and Oja Pada connotations.

.....(फ)लयोजना | उच्चाधिपतेरारंभकत्वम् | स्वोच्चराशिस्थितस्यारंभकत्वम् | स्वस्य उच्चत्वं वा कल्पनया उच्चगतत्वं वा यस्य कस्यचिदारंभकस्य उच्चत्वं वा |

The method of interpreting the results is: the lord of exaltation sign being the Arambhaka, a planet placed in the exaltation sign of the Pachaka being the Arambhaka, Pachaka placed in exaltation sign in the Rasi Chakra or in prepared (Graha) Chakras, or any planet who is exalted becoming the Arambhaka (– these dispositions indicate favourable results and Raja Yoga?)

NOTES: The manuscript has gaps at this important juncture where the author is going to explain the method of interpretation of the Dasa results. However, the following insights can be had from the text:

The following Dasas can give auspicious results and Raja Yogas:

(i) If the lord of exaltation sign of the Pachaka becomes the Arambhaka.

(ii) If a planet placed in the exaltation sign of the Pachaka becomes the Arambhaka.

(iii) The Pachaka being exalted in the Rasi Chakra or in prepared Chakras. I feel the author wants us to refer to the Graha Chakra here.

(iv) Any exalted planet becoming the Arambhaka.

Conversely, we can infer that the following Dasas can give difficulties to the native:

(i) If the lord of debilitation sign of the Pachaka becomes the Arambhaka.

(ii) If a planet placed in the debilitation sign of the Pachaka becomes the Arambhaka.

(iii) The Pachaka being debilitated in the Rasi Chakra or in the Graha Chakra.

(iv) Any debilitated planet becoming the Arambhaka.

अस्य स्फु(ट ग्रह रीत्या).....(स्वामिगुरुज्ञदृग्योगोद्वि)तीय इति भावलग्नसप्तमयोर्बलवतस्स्वीकारः | अस्यसूत्रस्यार्थः | अत्र स्वि(अधि/राशि)पतिगुरुबुधानां दृष्टियोगोद्वितीयबलमिति | तत्रोद्देशक्रमाद्दृष्टि(प्रा)धान्यं तदभावेयोगस्य | स्वामिदृष्टे....| तदभावे बुधदृष्टिर्ग्राह्या | ....योऽपि तथा | एवं प्रकारेण बलवद्राशिमारभ्य तत्तद्दशाक्रमेण क्रमोत्क्रमाभ्यां एकैकंवर्षं एकैकस्य कल्पइत्वा प्रागुक्तन्यायेन शुभमशुभंवा फलं वाच्यम् |

(Now, the method of Varshacharya will be explained?) Considering the Rasi Chakra, the second kind of strength mentioned in the Sutra **स्वामिगुरुज्ञदृग्योगोद्वितीयः** is to be applied to the Bhava Lagna and its 7th sign to initiate the Varshacharya. The meaning of this Sutra is - the aspect and conjunction of the sign lord, Jupiter and Mercury constitute the second type of strength. Here, as per the sequence mentioned, the priority is to be given to the aspect. Only when aspects are absent, conjunctions are to be considered. First, the aspect of the sign lord is to be considered. If that is absent, the aspect of Jupiter is to be considered. When that too is absent, the aspect of Mercury is to be considered. The sequence of preference in conjunctions is also to be similarly considered. In this way, starting from the stronger sign (between the Bhava Lagna and its 7th sign) and following the sequence of the respective Dasa in zodiacal or reverse order, the Varshacharya is to be taken one sign representing one year and the favourable and malefic results are to be predicted based on the rules explained before.

NOTES: It appears that the text is dealing with the method of Varshacharya after explaining the Bhava Lagna Karaka Dasa. We are told that the Varshacharya starts from the Bhava Lagna or its 7th sign, whichever is stronger, following the 2nd kind of strength of *Swamigurujna Drigyoga*. The hierarchical way to apply this Sutra is also explained. However, there is a practical problem here. In some cases, both the Bhava Lagna and its 7th house might not have this kind of strength. Then what should be done to determine the stronger between them? Because, unlike a conditional Dasa, Varshacharya is to be applied to all horoscopes. In such cases, I feel, this second kind of strength is to be applied to the Bhava Lagna Lord and to the lord of its 7th sign to determine the stronger between them. Then, the Varshacharya is to be initiated from the sign of the stronger lord. This is my opinion which has the support of another important Jaimini text 'Kalpalata'. My learned friend Shanmukha opines that this Sutra of second kind of strength is applicable only to the signs but not to the planets. Hence, he says that in the instance when the Bhava Lagna and its 7th are devoid of this strength, the Bhava Lagna itself is to be considered as the starting point.

In the present example horoscope, Bhava Lagna is Aquarius while its 7th sign is Leo. Neither Aquarius nor Leo fulfils the condition of Swamigurujna Drigyoga. Hence, to determine the stronger between them we should consider their lords Saturn and Sun. Saturn is placed in Sagittarius and receives the aspect of the sign lord Jupiter fulling the condition of Swami Drishti. Though, the 7th lord Sun also receives the aspect of Jupiter, the sign lord Mercury does not aspect the Sun. Hence, the Bhava Lagna Aquarius is stronger than its 7th sign and the Varshacharya should start from it. This is my opinion.

Next, we are asked to take the Varshacharya considering one sign for one year in the zodiacal or reverse order as per the respective Dasa. This suggests that the Varshacharya can be applied to any of the Dasas. Otherwise, it may mean that considering the odd and even nature of the initiating sign the Varshacharya shall move in zodiacal or reverse order.

The other possible interpretation would be - for each of the Bhava Lagna Karaka Dasas, consider the way the Dasa years are calculated in the zodiacal or reverse order from the Arambhaka to the Pachaka. Then, starting from the stronger sign between Bhava Lagna and its 7th, take the Varshacharya by considering one sign per year in the same zodiacal or reverse order. Interpret the results of Varshacharya by keeping the Pachaka in the respective sign in the year and considering his exaltation, debilitation, benefic and malefic nature etc.
It is said that the results of the Varshacharya are to be interpreted as explained before. Earlier, the author gives a statement that the Graha Chakra is to be applied for Varshacharya analysis. Therefore, we can experiment interpreting the Varshacharya results by blending the planetary positions in the Rasi Chakra and Graha Chakra for a particular sign ruling over particular year. This could be another way of interpreting the Varshacharya.

EXAMPLE HOROSCOPE-5

उदाहरणम् | गंगाधरभट्ट जातकम् | शकाब्दाः १५१२ | खरसंवत्सर वैशाखमासं तेदी २३ शुक्रवारं रात्रौ घटिकाः १० जनन कालः | | गंगाधरभट्टः | अत्र स्फुटग्रहाः | रवि | १|२३|१५|| चन्द्रः |५|९|१४|| कुजः |८|१९|८|| बुधः |२|..|..|| गुरुः |~~७~~(६)|४|३२|| शुक्रः |२|१८|५४|| शनिः |२|६|४४|| राहुः |२|१६|४४|| केतुः |८|१६|४४|| लग्नं कुंभः | भावलग्नं ~~वृषभः~~ कुंभः| कारको रविः | तत्सप्तमो गुरुश्च |
Another example horoscope will be discussed now. The native named Gangadhara Bhatta was born in the year Khara corresponding with the Saka year 1512, on the 23rd day of the month of Vaisakha, on a Friday, 10 Ghatis after Sunset. The planetary positions at the time of the native's birth are: the Sun - 1.23°.15', the Moon - 5.09°.14', Mars - 8.19°.08', Mercury - 2…°…',

Jupiter - 6.04°.32', Venus - 2.18°.54', Saturn - 2.06°.44', Rahu - 2.16°.44', and Ketu - 8.16°.44'. The Lagna is Kumbha. The Bhava Lagna is also Kumbha. Karaka is the Sun. The 7th planet from the Sun is Jupiter.

NOTES: The details given here match with the planetary positions between 1st and 3rd June 1591 AD corresponding to the Hindu calendar of Khara Samvatsara, Jyeshtha Shukla Dashami and Ekadashi respectively. The time of birth turns out to be almost 48 Ghatis after Sunrise which is about 12.15 AM. Position of the Moon in Virgo matches when 1st June is considered but Mercury would be in Taurus instead of Gemini. The degree-wise position of the Sun matches when 3rd June is considered and Mercury also moves into Gemini. However, Moon will be in Libra instead of Virgo. Nevertheless, 1st June is falling on a Friday as mentioned by our author while 3rd June is a Sunday. Though the Hindu calendar matches with the description in case of the year Khara, the lunar month does not match. The dates fall in the lunar month of Jyeshtha while the author has given it as Vaisakha. If the month is considered as Vaisakha, then the birth of the native turns out to be on 4th of May, 1591 AD at about 1.15 AM on Khara Vaisakha Shukla Ekadashi on a Friday. However, the position of the Sun and Mercury will be in Aries while Venus will be in Taurus which does not match with the description and discussion given here.

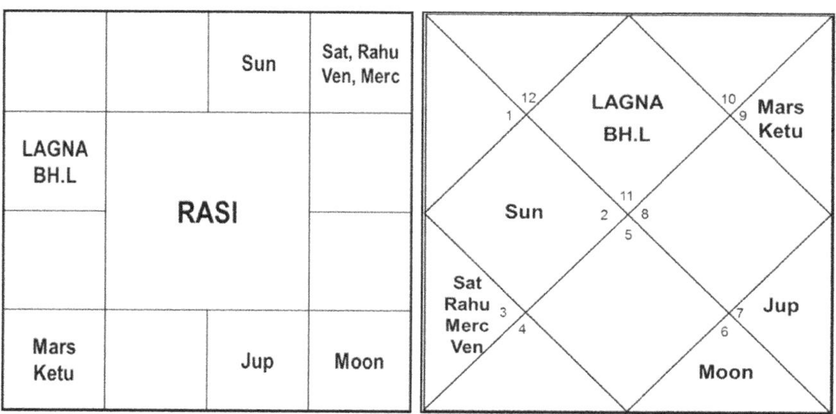

The Bhagakaladhika Karaka in this horoscope is the Sun. The native was born about 48 Ghatis after Sunrise. Now, counting 5 Ghatis for

each sign starting from the sign occupied by the Karaka Sun, the Bhava Lagna will fall in Aquarius. To determine the Karakas for the Bhava Lagna Karaka Dasa, we need to consider the Kendras of the Bhava Lagna and their lords. The Kendras of the Bhava Lagnas are Aquarius, Taurus, Leo and Scorpio while their lords are Saturn, Venus, Sun and Mars respectively. When counted from their respective signs, Saturn has moved 5 signs, Venus has moved 2 signs, and the Sun has moved 10 signs while Mars has moved 2 signs. Hence the first Karaka is the Sun.

Now, the 7th planet from the Sun as per the position in the Rasi Chakra will become the second Karaka. In the Rasi Chakra, the planetary sequence with reference to the Sun is – (i) Sun, (ii) Mercury, (iii) Rahu, (iv) Saturn, (v) Venus, (vi) Moon, and (vii) Jupiter. Hence, Jupiter will become the second Karaka. Between the two Karakas, the Sun is stronger as per the Naisargika strength and hence will become the first Pachaka while the other Karaka Jupiter will become the first Arambhaka.

राहुशनियोगात् बुधेनसहमिध्(थुन?)....कर्कटे शनिः । सिंहे शुक्रः । कुजसंबन्धात् केतुर्वृश्चिके कल्पनीयोवर्षसंख्यार्थम् । आरंभकत्वं तु यथास्थितस्यैवेतिसंप्रदायः ।

Because of the conjunction of Saturn and Rahu along with Mercury.....Saturn is to be placed in Cancer. Venus is to be placed in Leo. Because of his association with Mars, Ketu is to be placed in Scorpio for the purpose of counting the years. As an *Arambhaka*, however, the actual position of Ketu is to be considered. This is as per the hoary tradition.

NOTES: This is an example horoscope where the exception rules mentioned for the Saturn-Rahu and Mars-Ketu combination at Page 65 become applicable. As the Saturn-Rahu combination in Gemini has the Sun in the previous sign Taurus, Saturn is to be placed in the next sign in Cancer while Rahu should be retained in the actual sign Gemini. Saturn and Rahu have joined other planets Mercury and Venus in Gemini. Among them Mercury is the lord of Gemini, hence, should be placed in Gemini itself. The next planet Venus is to be placed in Leo after Saturn in Cancer. In the case of Mars-Ketu combination in Sagittarius, as there are no planets in the previous sign Scorpio, Ketu is to be placed in Scorpio. These modified positions of the planets are to be used in calculating the Dasa years only when they are considered as Pachakas. When these planets are considered as Arambhakas, their actual positions in the Rasi Chakra are to be considered.

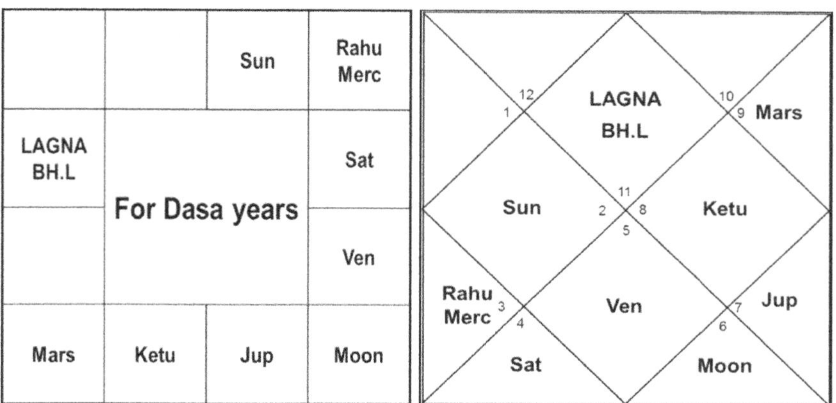

वर्षानयनम् | आरंभकस्यगुरोः ...(ओजराशौ स्थि)तत्वेन ग्रहवैषम्याच्च अनुलोमो ग्रहक्रमः | तदनुसारिकत्वात् पाचकस्यरवेरपि | ततश्च गुर्वादिरवेरष्टवर्षाणि | केत्वादिबुधस्य सप्त | कुजादि.....रव्यादिव्युत्क्रमेणशनेरेकादश | बुधादिशुक्रस्य त्रीणि | रह्वादिचन्द्रस्य चत्वारि | शन्यादिगुरोः पञ्च | शुक्रादिकुजस्य सप्त | चन्द्रादिकेतोरेकादश | आहत्य त्रिषष्टि......रि पुनरावृत्तौ गुर्वादिरवेरष्टौ एकसप्तति वर्षाणि |

Now, the method of deriving the Dasa years will be explained. From the *Arambhaka* Jupiter….as he is placed in an odd sign (*Grahavaishamya* also may mean odd numbered planets in the sign), the planetary sequence follows the normal zodiacal order. From the *Pachaka* Sun also, the same sequence is to be followed. Hence, from Jupiter to the Sun – 8 years; from Ketu (Mars?) to Mercury – 7 years; from Mars (Ketu?) to …..; from the Sun to Saturn in reverse order – 11 years; from Mercury to Venus – 3 years; from Rahu to the Moon – 4 years; from Saturn to Jupiter – 5 years; from Venus to Mars – 7 years; and from the Moon to Ketu – 11 years. This totals to 63 years….after this, the first Dasa of 8 years from Jupiter to the Sun is repeated and the total period equals to 71 years.

NOTES: As the Arambhaka Jupiter is placed in an odd sign Libra (the reason for using the word *Grahavaishamya* here is not clear. It may mean that Jupiter is the single planet in Libra, thus giving an odd number. It may also mean that Jupiter is the 7th planet in the sequence in the Rasi Chakra, which is an odd number. This needs more inputs and deliberations to reach a conclusion). Hence, the sequence of the Arambhakas is to be determined from Jupiter in the regular zodiacal order. Thus, the Arambhakas are - (i) Jupiter, (ii) Ketu, (iii) Mars, (iv) Sun, (v) Mercury, (vi) Rahu (vii) Saturn, (viii) Venus, and (ix) Moon. The sequence of the nine Pachakas is to be determined starting from the first Pachaka Sun in the zodiacal order, similar to the order followed for the Arambhakas. Thus, the nine Pachakas are – (i) Sun, (ii) Mercury, (iii) Rahu, (iv) Saturn, (v) Venus, (vi) Moon, (vii) Jupiter, (viii) Mars, and (ix) Ketu. Please note that the last two Pachakas should be Ketu first and Mars next. However, Mars is considered first and then Ketu. I could not understand the logic here. Possibility of some corruption in the manuscript here cannot be ruled out. Nevertheless, to explain the purport of the author, I am considering the sequence as mentioned in the text.

Arambhaka	Sign	Pachaka	Sign	Dasa Years
Jupiter	Libra	Sun	Taurus	8
Ketu	Sagittarius	Mercury	Gemini	7
Mars	Sagittarius	Rahu	Gemini	7
Sun	Taurus	Saturn	Cancer	11
Mercury	Gemini	Venus	Leo	3
Rahu	Gemini	Moon	Virgo	4
Saturn	Saturn	Jupiter	Libra	5
Venus	Gemini	Mars	Sagittarius	7
Moon	Virgo	Ketu	Scorpio	11
Jupiter	Libra	Sun	Taurus	8

The first Arambhaka Jupiter is in an odd sign Libra. Hence, counting from Jupiter to the first Pachaka Sun in zodiacal order the duration of the first Dasa will be of 8 years. The second Arambhaka Ketu also occupies an odd sign Sagittarius. Hence, counting from Ketu to the second Pachaka Mercury in zodiacal order, the second Dasa will be of 7 years duration. The third Arambhaka Mars is also placed in Sagittarius. Therefore, counting from Mars to the third Pachaka Rahu in zodiacal order, the duration of the third Dasa would be of 7 years. The fourth Arambhaka Sun is placed in an even sign Taurus. Hence, counting from the Sun to the sign occupied by the fourth Pachaka Saturn in the modified Chakra (Cancer) in anti-zodiacal order, the fourth Dasa would be a period of 11 years. The fifth Arambhaka Mercury is placed in an odd sign Gemini. Thus, counting from Mercury to the sign occupied by the fifth Pachaka Venus in the modified Chakra (Leo) in zodiacal order, the fifth Dasa will be of 3 years duration. The sixth Arambhaka Rahu is also placed Gemini. Hence, counting from Rahu to the sixth Pachaka Moon in zodiacal order, the duration of the sixth Dasa would be of 4 years. The seventh Arambhaka Saturn is also placed in Gemini. Thus, counting from Saturn to the seventh Pachaka Jupiter in zodiacal order, the seventh Dasa would be a period of 5 years. The eighth Arambhaka Venus also occupies Gemini. Therefore, counting from Venus to the eighth Pachaka Mars in zodiacal order, the eighth Dasa duration will be of 7 years. The ninth and last Arambhaka Moon is placed in an even sign Virgo. Hence, counting from the Moon to the sign occupied by the ninth Pachaka Ketu in the modified Chakra (Scorpio) in the anti-zodiacal order, the duration of the ninth Dasa is of 11 years. Thus, the total of these nine Dasas would be 63 years (8+7+7+11+3+4+5+7+11). After completion of the first cycle, the Dasas will be repeated again. Thus, the repetition of 8 years of the first Dasa from Jupiter to the Sun will complete 71 years of the native's age.

EXAMPLE HOROSCOPE-6

अथ राजयोगोदाहरणम् | अक्बरु जातकम् | शकाब्दाः १४६४ शुभकृत् संवत्सर आश्वियुजमासं १४ तेदि शनिवारं सूर्योदयादि जननकालः ४९|००| अक्बरुनाम्नोऽश्वपतेर्जननम् | स्फुटग्रहाः | लग्नम् | ४|१५|३५|| रविः |६|१४|१|| चन्द्रः |९|०|३४|| कुजः |८|२९|२|| बुधः |६|११|२३|| गुरुः |५|२९|२|| शुक्रः |५|९|२८|| शनिः |६|२०|२३|| राहुः | केतुः |

Now, some examples of Raja Yoga will be demonstrated. This horoscope belongs to the emperor Akbar. He was born in the year Shubhakrut corresponding to the Saka year 1464, on the 14th day of the month Ashviyuja, on a Saturday, 49 Ghatis after Sunrise. The longitudes of the Lagna and the nine planets at the time of the native's birth are: the Lagna - 4.15°.35', the Sun - 6.14°.01', the Moon - 9.00°.34', Mars - 8.29°.02', Mercury - 6.11°.23', Jupiter - 5.29°.02', Venus - 5.09°.28', Saturn - 6.20°.23', Rahu - 10…°…', Ketu - 04…°…'.

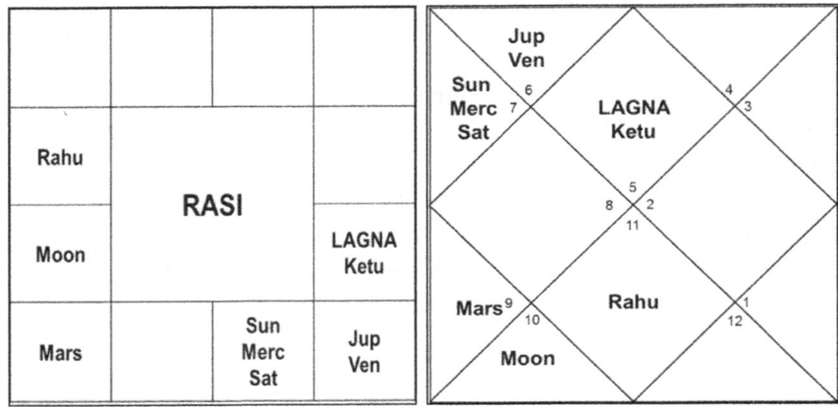

NOTES: The next three horoscopes have been presented to demonstrate the Upajeevya Raja Yogas based on the Atma and Amatya Karakas in the Rasi, Svamsa, Pada and Upapada Chakras. The birth details of this horoscope match with the date of 26th October 1542 AD at about 1.52 AM corresponding to the Hindu calendar Shubhakrut Samvatsara Ashviyuja Shukla Ashtami but the weekday is a Sunday instead of Saturday. The Sun would be in the 15th degree of Libra but the degrees of the Moon would not match.

अत्र अधिकभागकलौ कुजगुरू । पञ्चमनवमाधिपाभ्यां उपजीव्यौ इत्येकोमहान्योगः ।

Here, the planets having greater number of degree and minutes are Jupiter and Mars. In the form of 5th and 9th lords they have become *Upajeevyas* forming a great Yoga.

NOTES: Here, both the Jupiter and Mars attained greatest and equal number of degrees and minutes by occupying the 29°.02' in their respective signs. The author does not seem to consider the seconds (Viliptas or Vikalas) here to determine the Atma Karaka but considers both of them. Hence, the Svamsa Chakra has been prepared with two scenarios. The planetary positions are presented in italics font when Mars is considered as the Atma Karaka while the planetary positions are presented in normal font when Jupiter is the Atma Karaka. In fact, Jupiter has attained the Dwadasamsa of Leo while Mars has attained the Dwadasamsa of Scorpio.

Now, let us discuss about the first Upajeevya Yoga caused by the Bhagakaladhika Karakas Jupiter and Mars. Jupiter is the 5th lord while Mars is the 9th lord from the Janma Lagna. In the Rasi Chakra, Mars occupies the 5th house thereby providing the chance for the formation of Upajeevya Yogas. When the Svamsa Chakra is considered for the Mars, Jupiter is placed in Sagittarius in the 5th from Janma Lagna. Thus, an Upajeevya Yoga is formed because of the disposition of the Bhagakaladhika Karakas Jupiter and Mars who are also the 5th and 9th lords in the Rasi and Svamsa Chakras. This is the first Upajeevya Yoga.

रवेर्गुरुबुधोकुजोपजीव्यत्वादपरोमहान्योगः ।

The Sun having *Upajeevya* relationship with Jupiter and Mars will form another great Yoga.

NOTES: Now, let us take up the second Upajeevya Yoga. The Sun, who becomes the Atma Karaka being the Lagna lord, is the basis for the preparation of Pada Chakra. In the Pada Chakra, the Sun is placed in Sagittarius, the 5th house from the Janma Lagna where the Bhagakaladhika Karakas Mars and Jupiter are placed in the Rasi and Svamsa Chakras respectively. This forms the second Upajeevya Yoga.

अस्य लग्नसप्तमाधिपतेश्शनेश्च प....दि गताभ्यां गुरुकुजाभ्यां उपजीव्यत्वेन द्वौ महायोगौ । एवं च चतुर्णां योगानां संभवात्सिंहासनयोगः ।

Here, the 7th lord from Lagna, Saturn,….*Upajeevyatva* with Jupiter and Mars who are placed in…..two great Yogas are forming. Thus, four Yogas forming in this horoscope will generate *Simhasana Yoga*.

NOTES: The 7th lord from the Lagna, Saturn, is the Amatya Karaka who forms the basis of the Upapada Chakra. In the Upapada Chakra, Saturn is placed in Sagittarius, the 5th house from the Janma Lagna thereby paving way for the formation of Upajeevya Yogas. The third Upajeevya Yoga is formed between the Lagna lord Sun placed in Sagittarius in Pada Chakra and the 7th lord Saturn placed in Sagittarius in the Upapada Chakra. Further, Saturn also forms the fourth Upajeevya Yoga with the Bhagakaladhika Karakas Mars and Jupiter placed in Sagittarius in the Rasi and Svamsa Chakras respectively. Note that the Upajeevya Yogas with Mars and Jupiter are not considered as separate Yogas but as a single Yoga.

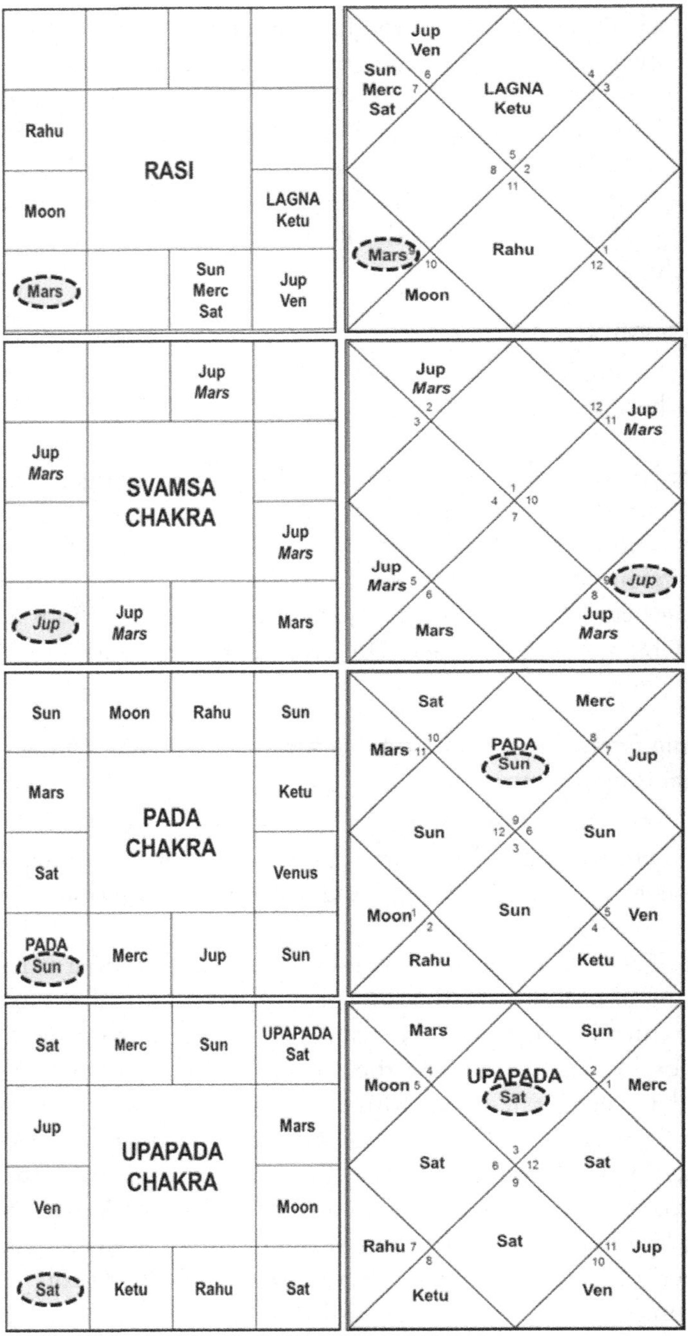

Rahu	**RASI**		
Moon			LAGNA Ketu
Mars		Sun Merc Sat	Jup Ven

Jup Ven 6
Sun Merc Sat 7
LAGNA Ketu
4 3
5 8 2 11
Mars 9 10
Moon
Rahu
1 12

		Jup *Mars*	
Jup *Mars*	**SVAMSA CHAKRA**		
			Jup *Mars*
Jup	Jup *Mars*		Mars

Jup *Mars* 2 3
12 11 Jup *Mars*
1 4 10 7
Jup *Mars* 5 6
Mars
9 *Jup*
8 Jup *Mars*

Sun	Moon	Rahu	Sun
Mars	**PADA CHAKRA**		Ketu
Sat			Venus
PADA Sun	Merc	Jup	Sun

Sat
Merc
Mars 10 11
PADA Sun
8 7 Jup
Sun 9 12 6 3
Sun
Moon 1 2
Sun
5 Ven
4
Rahu
Ketu

Sat	Merc	Sun	UPAPADA Sat
Jup	**UPAPADA CHAKRA**		Mars
Ven			Moon
Sat	Ketu	Rahu	Sat

Mars
Sun
Moon 5 4
UPAPADA Sat
2 1 Merc
Sat 3 6 12 9
Sat
Rahu 7 8
Sat
11 Jup
10
Ketu
Ven

The total Upajeevya Raja Yogas forming in this horoscope are thus four in number: (i) First formed because of Jupiter and Mars, (ii) Second formed because of the Sun with Mars and Jupiter, (iii) Third formed because of the Sun and Saturn (iv) Fourth formed because of Saturn with Mars and Jupiter. This results in the formation of a Simhasana Yoga or the Yoga for emperorship. It is to be noted that the author is considering the four Karakas – Atma Karaka, Amatya Karaka, Lagna lord and the 7th lord – for Upajeevya analysis.

रवियोगापेक्षया शानेः षष्ठगतत्वेन च नित्ययोगकारकत्वेऽपि...गे कर्तृत्वेन न दोषः | यद्यपि गुरोरष्टमाधिपतित्वेन एक योग(भंग?)दत्वं तथापि सिंहादि षष्ठगतत्वेन पञ्चमस्यैव प्राधान्यमिति न दोषः |

When compared with the Yoga involving Sun, Saturn attaining the 6th placement (6th lordship?), and also, though he is always a Yoga Karaka…..is generated by him, there is no blemish here. Though, Jupiter being the 8th lord may cause destruction of the Yoga (?), as Saturn (?) is in the 6th from Leo, the importance will be for the 5th (house position/lordship of Jupiter) only and hence, there is no blemish here.

NOTES: The author seems to be discussing the Raja Yoga cancellation in this part of the text. However, it is very difficult to comprehend because of the gaps in the manuscript. The author seems to refer to the 6th and 8th house lordships of Saturn and Jupiter respectively which can act as hindrances for the Raja Yoga. He further says that because of some reason this negative impact would not manifest.

EXAMPLE HOROSCOPE-7

एवमुदाहरणांतरम् | शकाब्दाः १५१३ खरसंवत्सर पौषमासं ८ तेदि उदयादि जननकालघटिकाः ३७|० सहजानि नाम्नोऽश्वपतेर्जननम् | स्फुटग्रहाः | रविः (|९|६|४३)|| चन्द्रः | ९|१९|२१|| कुजः |११|१३|४०|| बुधः |९|१४|३५|| गुरुः |~~२४२~~(७)|२४|१७|| शुक्रः |८|२|४६|| शनिः |२|१|११|| राहुः |२|१७|२६|| केतुः |८|१७|२६|| लग्नम् | ५|८|३७||

Another example for Raja Yoga is explained now with the horoscope of Shah Jahan (named here as Sahajani). He was born in the year Khara corresponding to the Saka year 1513, on the 8th day of the month Pausha, 37 Ghatis after Sunrise. Longitudes of the Lagna and the nine planets at the time of the native's birth are: the

Lagna - 5.08°.37', the Sun – (9.06°.43'), the Moon - 9.19°.21', Mars - 11.13°.40', Mercury - 9.14°.34', Jupiter - 7.24°.17', Venus - 8.02°.46', Saturn - 2.01°.11', Rahu - 2.17°.26', and Ketu - 8.17°.26'.

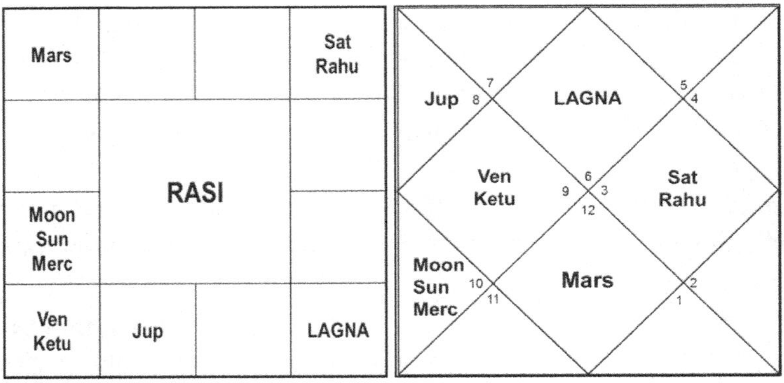

Mars			Sat Rahu
	RASI		
Moon Sun Merc			
Ven Ketu	Jup		LAGNA

Jup 7 8 LAGNA 5 4

Ven Ketu 9 6 3 12 Sat Rahu

Moon Sun Merc 10 11 Mars 2 1

NOTES: Longitude of the Sun is not given in the description. However, in view of the 8th day of the month and the Moon's position in Capricorn mentioned in the description, the Sun's position in the 7th degree of Capricorn is considered to determine the date. The birth details matched with the date 15th January 1592 AD at about 9.46 PM corresponding with the Hindu calendar Khara Samvatsara Pushya Masa Shukla Pratipat. To keep the Sun in the 8th degree the next day of 16th January would have to be considered, but the Moon would move into Aquarius on that day.

अधिकभागकलस्यगुरोः तदमात्यस्यचन्द्र.....(पञ्चमन)वमाभ्यां गुरुबुधाभ्यामुपजीव्यत्वेन महायोगौ द्वौ | एवं चतुर्णांसंभवे सिंहासनयोगः |

The Bhagakaladhika Karaka in this Chakra Jupiter and his Amatya the Moon ….Jupiter and Mercury attaining *Upajeevyatva* in the 5th and 9th, two great Yogas are forming in this Chakra. In this way, as four great Yogas are forming here, this generates a *Simhasana Yoga.*

NOTES: In this Chakra Jupiter is the Bhagakaladhika Atma Karaka while the Moon is the Amatya Karaka. Similarly, Mercury is the Lagna lord and hence Atma Karaka while Jupiter being the 7th lord is the Amatya Karaka. Here also, we are told that four Upajeevya Yogas are formed. Let us examine them. Among the Karakas, the Moon and Mercury are placed in Capricorn in the 5th house from the Janma Lagna in Rasi Chakra thereby paving the way for the Upajeevya Yogas.

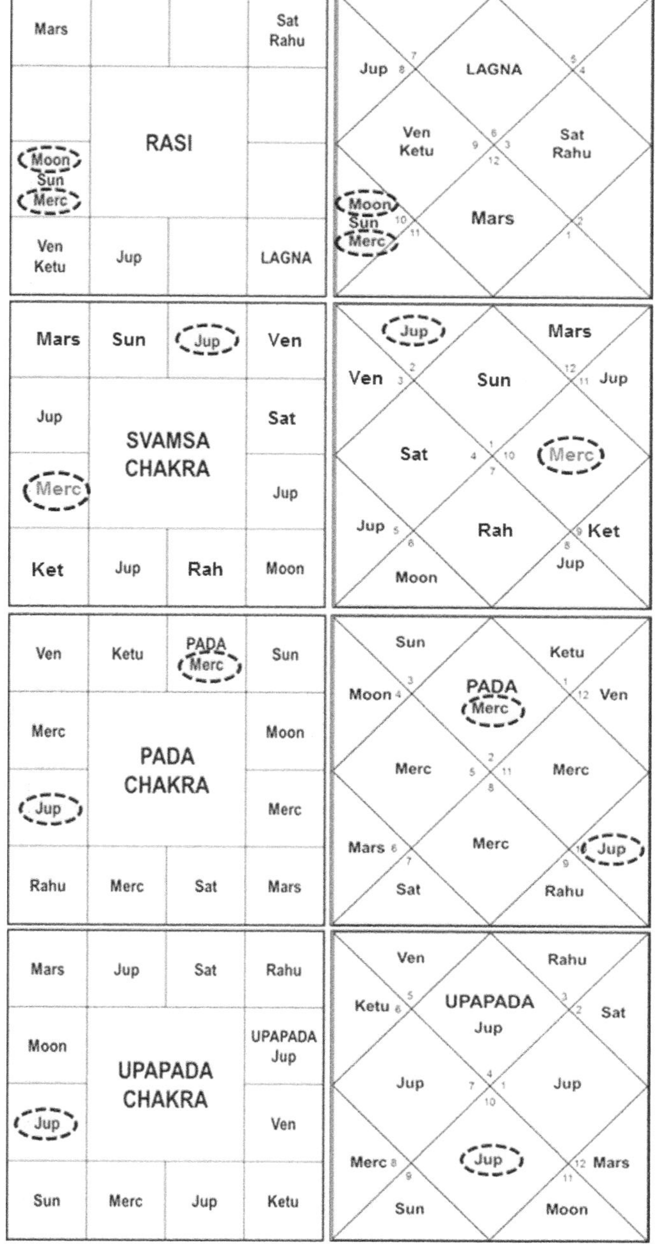

Firstly, the Bhagakaladhika Atma Karaka Jupiter occupies Capricorn in the Pada Chakra, forming the first Upajeevya Yoga with the Amatya Karaka Moon in the Rasi Chakra. Secondly, Mercury, the Atma Karaka being the Lagna Lord, occupies Capricorn in the Svamsa Chakra forming the second Upajeevya Yoga with the Amatya Karaka Moon placed in the Rasi Chakra. Thirdly, the Amatya Karaka Jupiter being the 7th lord from the Lagna occupies Capricorn in the Pada Chakra and Upapada Chakras where the Atma Karaka Lagna lord Mercury is placed in the Rasi Chakra. Fourthly, another Upajeevya Yoga is forming in Taurus in the 9th house from the Janma Lagna because of the placement of Jupiter in Taurus in the Svamsa Chakra and Mercury in Taurus in the Pada Chakra. The total Upajeevya Raja Yogas forming in this horoscope are therefore four in number: (i) First formed because of Jupiter and Moon, (ii) Second formed because of the Moon and Mercury, (iii) Third formed because of Jupiter and Mercury in Capricorn (iv) Fourth formed because of Jupiter and Mercury in Taurus. Thus, four Upajeevya Yogas are forming in this horoscope resulting in a Simhasana Yoga.

यद्यपि बुधस्य अधिकभागकलापेक्षया षष्ठं कल्पनया चाष्ट......(सं)बन्धोधिकयोगस्तथापि प्रकारांतरयोगत्वान्नदोषः । राजत्वरिक्तत्वयोस्सहानवस्थानात् । एवं रिक्तत्वमेवास्तु न राजत्वमितिवाच्यं । तदपेक्षया रा.....ति शुक्रकेतुयोगदांतर्भावात् ॥

Though, Mercury is placed in the 6th (in the synthetic Chakras) from the *Bhagakaladhika* Karaka Jupiter, the eighth.....association is a Yoga, further, as it generates another Yoga, it does not cause a blemish. This is because both Raja Yoga (Yoga for prosperity and rulership) and Rikta Yoga (Yoga for penury) would not happen simultaneously. If this is so, it should be said that only Rikta Yoga has formed and not the Raja Yoga. With reference to that....because the Venus and Ketu conjunction forms a Yogada combination.

NOTES: This portion of the text is highly incomprehensible because of the gaps in the manuscript. The author seems to be discussing about the negative factors in the four Upajeevya Yogas forming in this horoscopes and their nullifications and exceptions. While discussing the negative factors associated with Mercury, he seems to say that Mercury forms a part of the Argala Yoga being placed in the 2nd to the Yogada Venus-Ketu combination that aspects the Lagna and hence will give benefic results only. It is interesting to note that this discussion is being carried out for the horoscope of Shah Jahan who is said to have suffered incarceration and pathetic circumstances to the end of his life.

EXAMPLE HOROSCOPE-8

उदाहरणम् | औरंगजेबु जातकम् | शकाब्दाः १५४० कालयुक्ति संवत्सर आश्वयुजि २~~३~~(९) तेदि उदयादि जननकालः ५५|०| अवरंगजेबु नाम्नोऽश्वपतेर्जननम् | स्फुटग्रहाः | लग्नं |०|५|०|| रविः |~~५~~(६)|२८|२१|| चन्द्रः | कुजः |४|१५|६|| बुधः |६|१०|१३|| गुरुः |१०|१०|१३|| शुक्रः || शनिः || राहुः || केतुः ||

Another example horoscope is explained now to demonstrate the Raja Yogas. This Chakra belongs to Aurangzeb who was born in the year Kalayukti corresponding to the Saka year 1540, on the 29th day of the month Ashviyuja, 55 Ghatis after the Sunrise. The longitudes of the Lagna and the nine planets at the time of the native's birth are: the Lagna - 0.05°.00', the Sun – ~~5~~(6).28°.21', the Moon – (4)…, Mars - 4.15°.06', Mercury - 6.10°.13', Jupiter - 10.10°.13', Venus – (8)…, Saturn – (1)…, Rahu – (9)…, and Ketu – (3)….

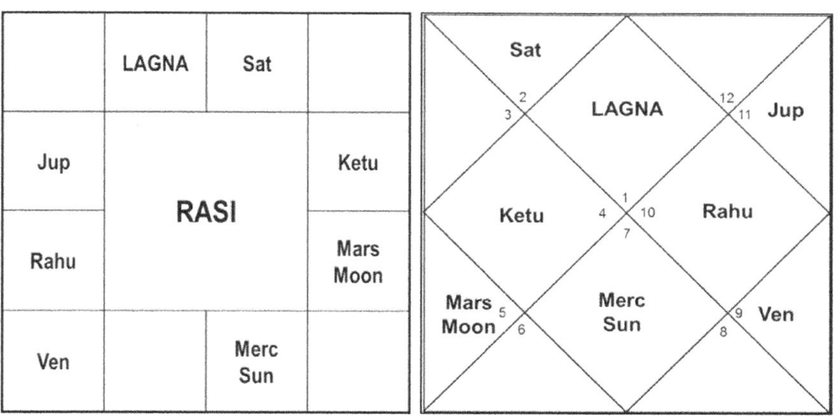

NOTES: The manuscript reads as 23rd day of the month of Ashviyuja while the Sun's position is mentioned in the 29th degree. Hence, I think there is some mistake in the manuscript and hence 29th day is to be considered instead of 23rd. Position of the Sun in Virgo appears also to be a mistake when we go through the discussion in the following lines. Also, in the month of Ashviyuja, the Sun will be placed in Libra. The planetary positions on the date 9th November 1618 AD at about 4.15 PM matched with the description given here and falls on Kalayukti Samvatsara Ashviyuja Masa Krishna Ashtami, on a Friday.

अधिकभागकलस्यरवेर्नवमशुक्रोपजीव्यं तदमात्यस्य सप्तमपञ्चमगत.......एतावान् ग्रन्थः उपलब्धः ।

The *Bhagakaladhika* Karaka Sun forms the *Upajeevya* Yoga with the Venus placed in the 9th and his Amatya ...with the planets placed in the 7th and 5th ......the manuscript is available up to this portion.

NOTES: In this horoscope, the Bhagakaladhika Atma Karaka is the Sun. The Amatya Karaka seems to be Mars. Similarly, being the Lagna lord Mars happens to be the Atma Karaka while Venus, the 7th lord, is the Amatya Karaka.

In the Svamsa Chakra, the Atma Karaka Sun is placed in Sagittarius which happens to be the 9th house from the Janma Lagna occupied by Venus in the Rasi Chakra, the 7th lord and Amatya Karaka, forming the first Upajeevya Yoga. The manuscript ends here abruptly after referring to the 5th and 7th houses from the Lagna. However, we can deduce the other Upajeevya Yogas from our understanding on the subject. In the Rasi Chakra, the Amatya Karaka Mars is placed in Leo in the 5th house from the Janma Lagna. Venus occupies Leo in the Upapada Chakra forming the second Upajeevya Yoga. The Atma Karaka Sun placed in Sagittarius in the Svamsa Chakra forms the third Upajeevya Yoga with the Lagna lord and Bhagakaladhika Amatya Karaka Mars who occupies Sagittarius in the Pada Chakra. Finally, the fourth Upajeevya Yoga is formed by the placement of Lagna lord Mars in Sagittarius in the Pada Chakra which happens to be occupied by the Amatya Karaka Venus in the Rasi Chakra in the 9th house from the Lagna. The total Upajeevya Raja Yogas forming in this horoscope also are four in number: (i) First formed between the Sun and Venus in Sagittarius, (ii) Second formed between the Sun and Mars in Sagittarius, (iii) Third formed between Venus and Mars in Leo (iv) Fourth formed between Venus and Mars in Sagittarius. Thus, four Upajeevya Yogas are forming in this horoscope resulting in a Simhasana Yoga.

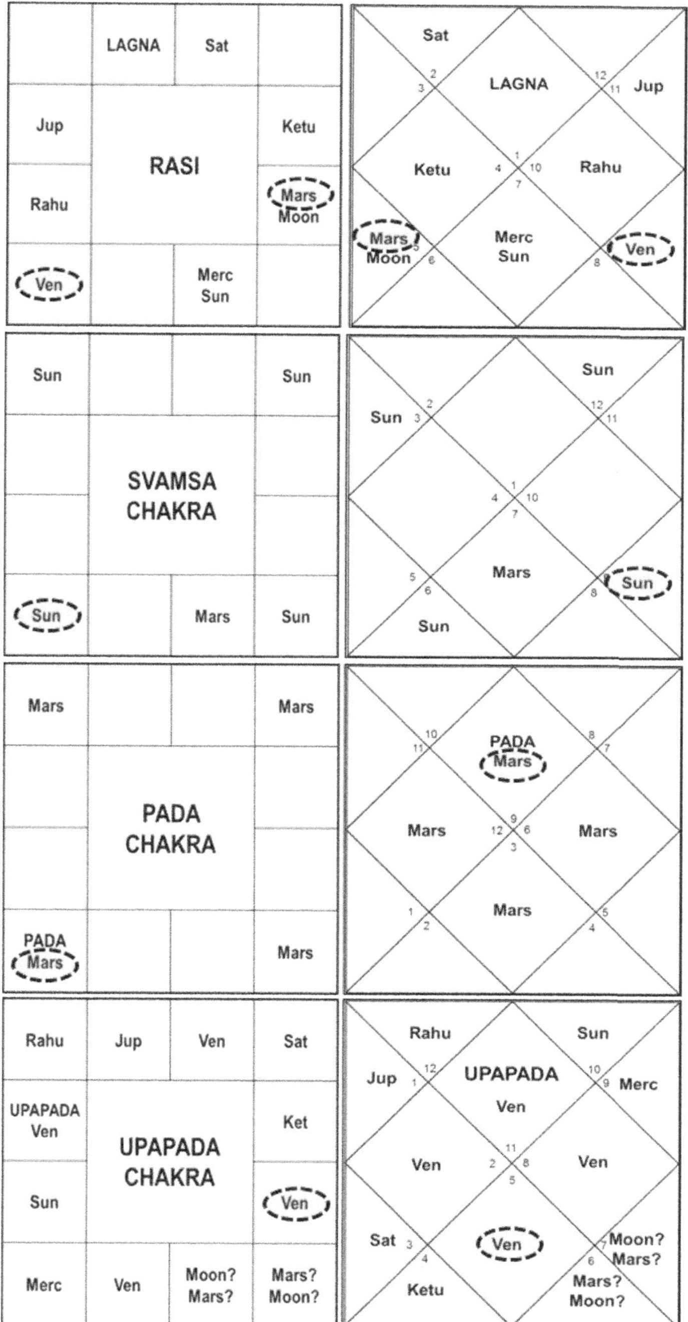

LAGNA
Sat
Jup
RASI
Ketu
Rahu
Mars
Moon
Ven
Merc
Sun
Sat
LAGNA
Jup
Ketu
Rahu
Mars
Moon
Merc
Sun
Ven
Sun
Sun
SVAMSA CHAKRA
Sun
Mars
Sun
Sun
Sun
Mars
Sun
Sun
Mars
Mars
PADA CHAKRA
PADA
Mars
Mars
PADA
Mars
Mars
Mars
Mars
Rahu
Jup
Ven
Sat
UPAPADA
Ven
UPAPADA CHAKRA
Ket
Sun
Ven
Merc
Ven
Moon?
Mars?
Mars?
Moon?
Rahu
Sun
Jup
UPAPADA
Ven
Merc
Ven
Ven
Sat
Ven
Moon?
Mars?
Ketu
Mars?
Moon?

पुस्तकमिदं श्रीमदस्मद्गुरूणां श्रीपादवेंकटरमणदैवज्ञशर्मणां पुस्तकं दृष्ट्वा विलंबि मार्गशीर्ष बहुल तृतीया इन्दुवासरे समाप्तिमानीतम् ।

On the 3rd Tithi of the dark fortnight of Margashirsha month in the year Vilambi, on a Monday, writing of this book has been finished by copying from a manuscript of my revered Guru Sri Sripada Venkataramana Daivajna Sharma.

NOTES: This date turns out to be 29th December, 1958. Exactly 60 years later, in the same Vilambi Samvatsara, I have attempted to bring this manuscript out for the benefit of the general public. We are forever indebted to this great Guru Sriman Madhura Krishnamurthy Sastry garu for all the pains he had taken to preserve and propagate the Jaimini Jyotisha.

-|| श्री कृष्णार्पणमस्तु ||-

1. Period of the author

This partial manuscript has eight horoscopes used to demonstrate various concepts. The birth years in CE of the natives are respectively: 1608, 1621, 1606, 1607, 1591, 1542, 1592, and 1618. The latest among them is horoscope-2 belonging to the year 1621 CE. Thus, we can safely presume that our author might have lived in the 17th century.

2. Style of mentioning the birth date

The author has referred to the day of birth in terms of the number of days completed in the solar month after the Sun entered into the sign while retaining the name of the month of the Amanta Masa of the lunar calendar. This would normally match with the degree occupied by the Sun in the respective sign.

3. Hora Lagna calculation

In the process of calculating the Hora Lagna the author considers the fixed duration of 2½ Ghatis as a Hora. Based on the odd and even nature of the Janma Lagna the counting is to be done in zodiacal or reverse order from the Lagna considering one sign for one Hora. The sign thus arrived for the time of birth will be the Hora Lagna.

4. Ghati Lagna calculation

The process of determining Ghati Lagna (or Ghatika Lagna) seems to be different from other treatises in one aspect. Normally, irrespective of the odd and even nature of the Janma Lagna, Ghati Lagna is determined by counting one sign for one Ghati in zodiacal order up to the time of native's birth. In the example horoscopes of this work, the reckoning is done in anti-zodiacal order when a node occupies the Lagna while normal zodiacal reckoning is followed when the Lagna is not occupied by a node, irrespective of the odd or even nature of the Lagna sign.

5. Sign and planetary Aspects

- A movable sign will aspect all the fixed signs excepting the one placed in its 2nd. A fixed sign will aspect all the movable signs excepting the one placed in its 12th. A dual sign will aspect all the other dual signs excepting itself.

- Aspects of signs are predominantly applied only when they are occupied by planets. Aspects of unoccupied signs are applicable only at a few instances including interpretation of transit results.
- When the signs are occupied by planets, the planetary Dasas are to be taken and the Argalas are to be judged by considering the planetary aspects.
- When the signs are unoccupied, the sign Dasas are to be taken and the Argalas are to be judged by considering the sign aspects.

6. Yogada planet - Raja & Bhagya Yogas

- The Yogada planets are determined from among the planets aspecting the three Lagnas – Janma Lagna, Hora Lagna and Ghatika Lagna – and the 7th house. Based on the maximum number of factors aspected and the strength of the sign occupied by the planets, only one sign is to be chosen and the planets placed in that sign are designated as the Yogadas to which the Argala analysis is applied. The application of the Sutra **न्यूना विबलाश्च** becomes pivotal in Yogada determination and Argala analysis.
- The aspect of exalted planets and planets having lordship over benefic houses from the Janma Lagna will cause benefic results.
- In contrary, the aspect of debilitated planets and planets having lordship over malefic houses from the Janma Lagna like the 6th, 8th and 12th houses will cause malefic results.
- The aspect of 5th lord causes Raja Yoga (political power) while the aspect of 9th lord causes Bhagya Yoga (wealth and fortune).
- Lordships of the planets are to be considered only from the Janma Lagna, not from any other Lagna. However, if the 7th house is stronger than the Lagna, it can be considered as the reference point.
- In some instances when the 7th house is also equally powerful or more powerful than the Janma Lagna, the aspect of 3rd lord from the Janma Lagna is also considered fortunate as he becomes the 9th lord from the 7th house.
- If the Lagna or the 7th house is aspected by a planet that has un-countered Argalas, the native will be blessed with *Sri* which means wealth and prosperity.

- When all the three Lagnas among the Janma Lagna, Hora Lagna and Ghatika Lagna are aspected by planets, the native will become a king. When two of them are aspected by planets, the native will not be a king but holds a position equal to a king.
- For the analysis of these Raja and Bhagya Yogas, only aspect of the planets are considered and not their placement, strictly following the principle of निध्यातुः.

7. Argalas and Virodha Argalas

- The Argala and Virodha Argala analysis is to be applied only to the sign occupied by the aspecting planet (Yogada). The remaining 11 signs would not come into the picture.
- The 4th, 2nd and 11th positions from the Yogada will form *Argalas* or interferers.
- The benefic and malefic results depend on the nature of the aspecting planet primarily. The Argalas will support the primary influence.
- If the aspecting planet is malefic in nature or debilitated, its aspect will cause malefic results primarily. Hence, the Argalas forming for such planet will support its malefic results. Contrarily, if the aspecting planet is benefic in nature or exalted, its aspect will cause benefic results and the Argalas for such planet will support the same.
- The planets placed in the *Virodha Argala* positions of 10th, 12th and 3rd signs will reverse the results of the aspecting planet – if the aspecting planet is to give benefic results, they convert it to malefic. If the aspecting planet is to give malefic results, they induce it to give benefic results.
- For the Argala signs of 4, 2 and 11, the signs 10, 12 and 3 will respectively become the Virodha Argala positions. Among them, the signs being week having less number of planets or debilitated planets etc. cannot exert their influence or Yoga. Contrarily, the signs being powerful being occupied by more number of planets or exalted planets etc. would exert their influence or Yoga.
- If both the Argala signs and their respective Virodha Argala signs are equal in strength, Bandhana Yogas are formed that cause bondage and incarceration to the native.

- Consider the trinal signs of the Argala and Viparita Argala positions. The planets placed in them support each other. For example, when we are looking for the Argala caused by the 2nd sign from the Yogada and its Virodha Argala caused by the 12th sign, we need to consider the planets posited in the trines to the 2nd – 6th and 10th signs, and to the 12th – 4th and 8th signs. The signs of a trine having exalted planets or strong planets or more number of planets will gain upper-hand over the other trine. In this context we should not think that 10th sign is one of the Virodha Argala positions or the 4th sign is one of the Argala positions. We are concerned here only with the Argala caused by the 2nd sign and Virodha Argala caused by the 12th sign. Similarly, other positions are to be judged. When both trines are equal in strength we are told that Mishra Argala will be formed.
- If more planets (not necessarily malefic planets, any planets will do) are present in the 3rd sign in comparison with the 11th sign from the Yogada, then also an Argala will form.
- Hence, even when the planets placed in the 11th house are few in number or weaker than the planets in the 3rd house, an Argala is formed and vice versa. The position of planets in the 7th house thus becomes irrelevant as it supports the Argala in any condition. This shows that Argala will form in any case when the 3rd house or 11th house is occupied by planets, except when equal numbers of planets or planets with equal strength are placed in them.
- If a planet occupies a trine from the sign where the aspecting planet is placed, a Viparita (Virodha) Argala is formed. Because of this, if the aspecting planet is to give benefic results, they will get modified into malefic results. If the aspecting planet is to give malefic results, contrarily, benefic results will get manifested.
- When one of the two trinal signs of the aspecting planet is occupied by planets, then only Viparita Argala is formed. If the two trinal signs have equal number of planets a Bandhana Yoga is formed which causes bondage to the native. When the two trines have unequal number of planets, the question of this Virodha Argala does not arise.

- This trinal rule of the Sutra *Viparitam Ketoh* is also to be judged with other Argala positions using the rule *Nanyuna Vibalashcha.*

8. Calculating the Dasa duration

- In general, the Dasa durations of sign Dasas are calculated following the rule *Nathamtah Samah* counting from the Dasa sign to its lord in zodiacal order for odd signs and anti-zodiacal order for even signs.
- For the Drik Dasa, when a node is placed in the Janma Lagna, the above order gets reversed – counting is done from the Dasa sign to its lord in anti-zodiacal order for odd signs and in zodiacal order for even signs.
- In the Drik Dasa, when the Janma Lagna is not occupied by nodes, the counting is done in zodiacal order for all the signs irrespective of their odd and even nature.
- If the Dasa sign lord is placed in the Dasa sign itself, the Dasa years are to be counted from the Dasa sign to the sign occupied by a planet immediately placed behind, as per zodiacal or reverse counting following the Dasa rules.
- In the case of planetary Dasas like the Bhava Lagna Karaka Dasa the counting is to be done from the Arambhakas to their respective Pachakas following the zodiacal or reverse order based on the odd or even nature of the signs occupied by the Arambhakas.

9. Drik Dasa - Calculation

- The Drik Dasa is applied to predict the timing the results of Yogada and Argala analysis.
- The Drik Dasa starts from the 9th house of the stronger between the Lagna and the 7th house.
- The entire Drik Dasa of the 12 signs is divided into three portions of four signs each as per the Sutra **कुजादि त्रिकूट पदक्रमेण दृग्दशा**. Here, the expression *Trikoota Pada Krama* seems to have been interpreted in this way of dividing the Dasa into three groups having four signs each.
- Dasa duration of the Drik Dasa is to be calculated using the Sutra *Nathamtah Samah*. If there is no node in the Lagna, Udaya

Chakra is to be applied to derive the Dasa years and not the Prakruti Chakra.

- If the nodes are placed in the Lagna and the 7th house, the Dasa years are to be counted in zodiacal order for even signs and anti-zodiacal order for odd signs (Vikruti Chakra).
- In the Drik Dasa, the author has explained detailed Khanda analysis of a Dasa sign if it happens to be the 9th house from the Janma Lagna or the 7th house and has 12 years duration. However, we can experiment with all the Dasa signs.
- For the Khanda analysis, the Dasa duration is to be divided into four quarters (Khandas). The first quarter is to be assigned to the 9th house from the sign occupied by the main Drik Dasa sign lord. The subsequent quarters are to be assigned to the subsequent 10th, 11th and 12th houses respectively.
- Even for the quarters (Khandas), subdivisions can be made which are called as Bhuktis. There are two ways of doing this.
    - Firstly, the duration of the quarter is divided into three equal parts and assigned to the trines of the Khanda sign. For example, if we have to do Bhukti analysis of the Khanda (quarter) of Scorpio, the duration of Scorpio quarter is divided into three parts and assigned to the trines of Scorpio – Scorpio, Pisces and Cancer, called as Bhuktis.
    - The second way of deriving the Bhuktis is to consider the number of planets placed in the Khanda sign and divide the duration into so many parts. These Bhuktis will be assigned to the planets as per their descending order of the longitudes in the sign.
- The first method of Bhukti analysis can be applied when a sign has no planets or a single planet. The second method of Bhukti analysis can be applied to Khanda sign having two or more planets.

10. Drik Dasa - Interpretation

- The Drik Dasa of a sign that lodges a Lagna receiving the aspect of the Yogada planet will manifest the Yogada result.
- Raja Yoga will get manifested in the Drik Dasa of the sign occupied by the Yogada planet.

- Raja Yoga will also manifest in the Dasa of a sign aspected by the Yogada planet.
- If the Yogada planet is the 9th lord, the Dasa will make the native fortunate.
- During the Dasa of the sign having the 9th lords from the Janma Lagna and the 7th house (meaning, 9th lord and 3rd lord) in the 2nd house, fortune should be predicted to the native.
- Aspect of two benefic planets on the Dasa/Khanda sign ensures benefic results in the period.
- Note the planet placed in the Dasa/Khanda/Bhukti sign. If it happens to be the exaltation sign lord of the main Dasa lord, the Dasa lord becomes exalted and gives benefic results. The contrary applies to the debilitation sign lord. This concept is unique to Jaimini system and is a general rule applicable to all the Dasas.
- The Dasa/Khanda/Bhukti sign having the exaltation sign lord of the Dasa lord or any planet in exaltation, receiving the aspect of the Yogada will give great Raja Yoga.
- If the Khanda/Bhukti sign happens to be the debilitation sign of the Dasa lord, then bad results are to be predicted during such period. If two benefic planets aspect the Khanda sign at the same time, the native will have some comforts even during the unfortunate period.
- If the Dasa/Khanda/Bhukti sign has a malefic planet and its lord also joins a malefic planet, bad results are to be predicted during the period.
- If the Dasa/Bhukti/Khanda sign has the association of two or more malefic planets, unfavourable results are to be predicted in the period.
- If the Bhukti lord in the 2nd kind of Bhuktis joins his exaltation sign lord in the Khanda sign, then he becomes exalted and gives favourable results in that period.
- If the planet ruling over the Bhukti as per the 2nd method joins his debilitation sign lord in the Khanda sign, it gives debilitation results. In this case, if this Bhukti lord happens to be the debilitation sign lord of the main Dasa lord, then it results in double debilitation affects and gives severe malefic results.

11. Three Atma Karakas

There are three Atma Karakas – (i) the planet that has attained more number of degrees and minutes, (ii) the Sun, and (iii) the Lagna lord.

12. Four types of Chakras

The Chakras are of four types – (i) Svamsa Chakra based on Bhagakaladhika Karaka, (ii) Pada Chakra based on the Lagna Lord, (iii) Upapada Chakra based on the 7th lord, and (iv) Graha Chakra based on the Sun. The first three Chakras have similar method of preparation and they are used in Upajeevya Raja Yoga analysis.

13. Svamsa Chakra preparation

- Take the planet which attained greater number of degrees and minutes as Bhagakaladhika Atma Karaka and place him in the Dwadasamsa sign of the sign occupied by him in the Rasi Chakra.
- Also, place him in the other three Kendra signs of the Dwadasamsa sign.
- Thus, after keeping the Atma Karaka in the four Kendras, the remaining eight planets that attained lesser number of degrees and minutes than the Atma Karaka are to be placed in descending order in the remaining eight signs.
- In the 2nd and 3rd houses from the Atma Karaka, the first two planets from the eight should be placed. The 4th house will be occupied by the Atma Karaka himself. In the 5th and 6th signs, the next two planets are to be placed. In this way, the Svamsa Chakra will be prepared.
- Note that the longitudes of Rahu and Ketu are considered as-it-is, not in the reverse order from the end of the sign they occupy. Rahu is considered first and Ketu, who has the same longitude, is placed in the next possible sign in the Svamsa Chakra.

14. Pada Chakra preparation

- Count the number of signs the Lagna lord is placed from the Lagna. The sign arrived by counting the same number from the Lagna lord will give the Pada or Arudha.

- In the Pada Chakra, the Lagna lord is to be placed in the four Kendras of the Pada. In the intervening signs, other eight planets should be placed sequentially in the order they are placed from the Lagna lord in the Rasi Chakra. This forms the Pada Chakra.

15. Upapada Chakra preparation

- Count the number of signs the 7th lord is placed from the 7th house. The sign arrived by counting the same number from the 7th lord will give the Upapada.
- In the Upapada Chakra, the 7th lord is to be placed in the four Kendras of the Upapada. In the intervening signs, other eight planets should be placed sequentially in the order they are placed from the 7th lord in the Rasi Chakra. This forms the Upapada Chakra.

16. Interpretation of the three Chakras

- Consider the actual position of the Bhagakaladhika Atma Karaka in the Rasi Chakra as the reference point or Lagna in the Svamsa Chakra and judge the twelve bhavas based on the nature of planets placed in them in the Svamsa Chakra.
- Apply the Sutras mentioned for the Svamsa Chakra in the 2nd quarter of the 1st chapter of the Jaimini Sutras starting with the Sutra अथ स्वांशो ग्रहाणां.
- The Dwadasamsa signs of the planets in the Svamsa Chakra as considered for the Svamsa Chakra Karaka Dasa is to be applied to know the good and bad results. This means, ignoring the sign occupied by the planets in the Rasi Chakra and considering their degrees and minutes in the signs they occupy in the Svamsa Chakra, their respective Dwadasamsa signs are to be determined. If the Dwadasamsa signs are occupied by malefic planets in the Rasi Chakra malefic results are to be predicted. Contrarily, if the Dwadasamsa signs are occupied by benefic planets in the Rasi Chakra, favourable results are to be predicted.
- In the Pada Chakra, the Pada is to be considered as the Lagna.

- The Upapada will be the Lagna of the Upapada Chakra from which the 12 Bhavas are to be judged.
- In the case of Svamsa Chakra, the planetary positions in a sign in the Svamsa Chakra, Rasi Chakra and Graha Chakra are to be blended to apply the results mentioned in the 2nd quarter.
- In the case of Pada Chakra, the planetary positions in the Svamsa Chakra, Pada Chakra, Rasi Chakra and Graha Chakra are to be blended to interpret the results mentioned in the 3rd quarter.
- In the case of Upapada Chakra, the planetary positions in the Svamsa Chakra, Pada Chakra and Upapada Chakra are to be considered along with those of the Rasi Chakra to apply the results mentioned in the 4th quarter. Note that the Graha Chakra has been excluded in this context.
- The rules mentioned in the previous sections will become applied to the subsequent sections. It means that the Sutras of the 2nd quarter are to be applied for interpreting Svamsa Chakra results. The Sutras of the 2nd and 3rd quarter are to be applied to the Pada Chakra. Finally, the Sutras of the 2nd, 3rd and 4th quarter are to be applied to the Upapada Chakra.
- The results of the Sutras dealing with Svamsa Chakra and Pada Chakra can be applied to both of them. Thus, the Sutras of 2nd and 3rd quarter can be applied to both Svamsa Chakra and Pada Chakra.

17. Graha Chakra

- Keeping the position of the Sun in the Rasi Chakra fixed, the remaining 8 planets are to be placed in sequential order in the 2nd, 3rd, 4th, 6th, 8th, 9th, 10th and 12th houses from the Sun. The 5th, 7th and 11th houses are to be filled with Jupiter, Venus and Saturn respectively.
- In the Graha Chakra or the Ravi Chakra, the position of the Sun in the Rasi Chakra is to be fixed and the 12 houses are to be studied with reference to the Sun.
- The process of preparing this Graha Chakra is different from the Graha Chakra mentioned at the Karakas.
- Graha Chakra is to be employed in Varshacharya analysis.

18. The other Karakas and Sthira Karakas

- The three Atma Karakas have three Amatya Karakas. The planet having immediately lesser degrees and minutes than the Bhagakaladhika Atma Karaka is his Amatya Karaka. In the case of the Sun, the Moon is the Amatya Karaka. For the Lagna lord, the 7th lord will be the Amatya Karaka.
- In the case of Svamsa Chakra, the seven planets in descending order of their longitudes will form the seven Karakas.
- In the case of Pada Chakra also, we are asked to consider the 3rd lord as the Bhratru Karaka. Similarly, we have to consider the 4th, 5th and 6th lords as Matru, Putra and Jnati Karakas respectively. However, the 7th lord is considered as Amatya Karaka instead of Kalatra Karaka while the Karakatva of the 2nd lord remains unclear.
- Putra Karaka is also considered as the Pitru Karaka.
- From the eighth to the twelfth houses, the well-noted significations should be considered in the Svamsa Chakra and Pada Chakra. The eighth stands for *Nidhana* or *Mrutyu* (death). The ninth stands for *Guru* (preceptor) and *Dharma* (religious merit), tenth for *Ajna* (executive power) and *Karma* (work or job), eleventh for *Labha* (gains) and the twelfth house stands for *Vyaya* (expenses). The significations for these houses in the Graha Chakra are separately mentioned in the next five Sutras.
- In the Graha Chakra, from the 8th house and Mars the four relatives - one's sisters, mother, younger brother of one's wife, own younger brothers – are to be judged.
- From Mercury and the 9th house maternal relations like maternal uncles and maternal aunts, and others who are equal to one's mother are to be judged.
- From Jupiter and the 10th house, primarily the native's grandfather and great-grandfather, husband or lord, and sons are to be judged.
- From Venus and the 12th house one's wife, in-laws, one's own parents, own maternal grandparents are to be judged.
- From the 11th house and Saturn, the matters related to the elder brothers of the native are to be judged.
- The Graha Chakra mentioned here with the planetary positions – Sun, Moon, Mars, Mercury, Jupiter, Saturn, Venus, Mars,

Mercury, Jupiter, Saturn, and Venus – appears to be different from the Graha Chakra erecting method explained earlier.

- Apparently, this Graha Chakra is used to predict the Arishtas (dangers) to the respective relatives of the native and to derive the Dasa to time the calamitous events.

19. Svamsa Chakra Karaka Dasa - Calculation

- This is a planetary Dasa based on the Svamsa Chakra. The author has not mentioned the name of this Dasa. I would like to refer it as **Svamsa Chakra Karaka Dasa** until a proper name of this Dasa comes to the fore from other manuscripts or treatises.
- This Dasa starts from the Bhagakaladhika Atma Karaka from his first position in the Svamsa Chakra and ends with the planet placed in the 12th from his first position.
- The planets that cause the Dasa results or that rule over the Dasas are named as the Pachakas.
- The method of deriving Dasa years is based on the position of planets in the Svamsa Chakra. Ignoring the actual sign a planet occupies, consider the sign it occupies in the Svamsa Chakra and determine the resultant Dwadasamsa sign of that sign based on the degrees and minutes of the planet. After this, the duration of years of the planet Dasa is determined by counting from the resultant sign to the sign occupied by its lord (in the Rasi Chakra) following the zodiacal or reverse order based on the odd or even nature of the Dwadasamsa sign. Only for the first Dasa of the Atma Karaka, his actual position in the Rasi Chakra is to be considered to find out the resultant Dwadasamsa sign.
- Varga Chakras of modern age are not used here. Planetary aspects, conjunctions, Dasa years and so on are considered from the Rasi Chakra only.

20. Svamsa Chakra Karaka Dasa - Interpretation

- The results attributed to the presence of the Atma Karaka in the 12 signs in Svamsa in the 2nd quarter of Chapter 1 of the Jaimini Sutras can be applied during the first Dasa or subsequent Dasas of the Atma Karaka. The time of fructification of the results can be at the end of the Dasa.

- The sign occupied by the Dasa lord in the Svamsa Chakra is to be considered as the Lagna and the relative position of planets in the Rasi Chakra and the Svamsa Chakra from that sign are to be blended to give the interpretation.
- The Bhavas occupied by malefic planets in Rasi and Svamsa Chakras with respect to the above Lagna would indicate bad results to such Bhavas during the period.
- The benefic and malefic nature of the Svamsa sign occupied by the Dasa lord will have a prominent influence on the favourable and unfavourable nature of the results experienced by the native.
- If the Dwadasamsa sign of the Dasa lord is occupied by malefic planets in the Rasi Chakra, the Dasa will give malefic results.
- Two or more malefic planets influencing the Dwadasamsa sign of the Dasa lord indicate death of the native's kith and kin, and loss of wealth.
- If the Dwadasamsa sign of the Dasa lord is occupied by two or more benefic planets and/or exalted planets, the Dasa will give exceedingly favourable results.
- If the Dasa lord from his position in the Svamsa Chakra has Upajeevya Yoga with the Atma Karaka or Amatya Karaka posited in the 5th or 9th signs from the Janma Lagna in the Rasi Chakra, there will be Raja Yoga.
- If the Dasa lord has Upajeevya Yogas with the Karakas by being placed in the immediately adjacent signs, then a mere Dhana Yoga will form.
- When there is no Upajeevya Yoga, then the Dasa of a malefic Atmakaraka who has malefic planets in his Dwadasamsa sign in Rasi Chakra would cause malefic results only.
- A general rule is that the junction between any two Dasas would cause unfavourable results.
- The Dasas of planets coming in the 6th, 8th and 12th in the sequence would be generally unfavourable in nature.
- The Dasa being 6th or 8th or 12th in the sequence will nullify even the powerful good Yogas and make the native experience ordinary comforts.

- Presence of exalted planets in the 8th and 2nd signs from the Dasa lord in the Svamsa Chakra would bless the native with immense wealth during the Dasa.
- The Dasa of a planet who occupies exaltation sign in Svamsa Chakra would cause benefic results like gain of wealth and so on.
- The 2nd sign from the Dasa lord occupied by malefic planets in Svamsa and Rasi Chakras indicates death of the native's kith and kin, and disturbance in family.
- Find out the 8th lord from the Bhagakaladhika Karaka in the Rasi Chakra. If in the Svamsa Chakra, the Dasa lord happens to occupy the Dwadasamsa sign of such 8th lord, the Dasa would give malefic results.

21. Atmano Bhavapamsa Dasa

- Considering the nature of the sign occupied by the Atma (Bhagakaladhika Karaka) and the nature of the Dwadasamsa sign occupied by the lord of the 8th house from the Atma, the longevity of the native is to be decided as explained below.
- For a movable sign the movable, fixed and dual signs; for a fixed sign the dual, movable and fixed signs; for a dual sign the fixed, dual and movable signs respectively form the *Jiva*, *Roga* and *Mruti*. Here, *Jiva* means long span of life, *Roga* means medium span of life, and *Mrutyu* means short span of life.
- Starting the Dasas from the Dwadasamsa sign of the 8th lord from the Atma Karaka, the native's death is to be predicted in the Dasa of the sign aspected by the 8th lord.

22. Calculation of the Bhava Lagna

Starting from the sign occupied by the Bhagakaladhika Atma Karaka, arrive at the Lagna by counting one sign for every 5 Ghatis up to the time of birth in regular zodiacal order. This will give the Bhava Lagna.

23. Bhava Lagna Karaka Dasa - Calculation

- After calculating the Bhava Lagna, consider the four Kendras of the Bhava Lagna. Among the lords of these four Kendras, the one who has moved more number of signs when counted from his sign will be the Karaka.

- If the lords of the Kendras of Bhava Lagna are equal as per the above said criterion, the one who has moved more number of signs with reference to the Bhava Lagna is to be considered as the first Karaka.
- The seventh planet from such Karaka counted sequentially as per the planetary position in the Rasi Chakra is also a Karaka. Between the two Karakas, the planet who is intrinsically strong (Naisargika Bala) is called the Pachaka (Dasa lord). The other Karaka is called the Arambhaka (starter).
- The nine planets starting from the Arambhaka are to be written down in the order of their sequence in the Rasi Chakra in zodiacal order or reverse order based on the odd or even nature of the sign occupied by the Arambhaka.
- Similarly, the nine Pachakas are to be determined starting from the first Pachaka in the same sequence of the Arambhakas. This means, if the sequence of Arambhakas is determined by following zodiacal order, the sequence of Pachakas also follows the zodiacal order. If the sequence of the Arambhakas is determined following anti-zodiacal order, the Pachaka sequence is also to be determined by anti-zodiacal order.
- Counting from the sign occupied by the first Arambhaka to the sign occupied by the first Pachaka in zodiacal or reverse order based on the odd or even nature of the sign occupied by the Arambhaka, the duration of the first Dasa is to be determined. The same procedure is to be applied to determine the duration of the next eight Dasas.
- There are some exceptions to calculate the duration of the Dasa years when Rahu joins Saturn or Ketu joins Mars.
    - If the previous sign from the sign occupied by Rahu-Saturn or Ketu-Mars is empty then Rahu or Ketu should be placed in the previous sign.
    - If the previous sign is not empty, Rahu or Ketu should be placed in the same sign occupied by them but Saturn or Mars respectively should be placed in the next sign.
    - If the sign lord also joins them, he should be placed in the same sign.

- o If planets other than the sign lord also join Saturn-Rahu or Mars-Ketu, they should be placed in the signs next to Saturn or Mars respectively. Here, if more than one planet joins them, they should be placed as per their degree-wise position.
- These modified positions of the planets are to be used in calculating the Dasa years only when they are considered as Pachakas. When these planets are considered as Arambhakas, their actual positions in the Rasi Chakra are to be considered.

24. Bhava Lagna Karaka Dasa - Interpretation

The following Dasas can give auspicious results and Raja Yogas:

(i) If the lord of exaltation sign of the Pachaka becomes the Arambhaka.

(ii) If a planet placed in the exaltation sign of the Pachaka becomes the Arambhaka.

(iii) The Pachaka being exalted in the Rasi Chakra or in prepared Chakras. I feel the author wants us to refer to the Graha Chakra here.

(iv) Any exalted planet becoming the Arambhaka.

Conversely, we can infer that the following Dasas can give difficulties to the native:

(i) If the lord of debilitation sign of the Pachaka becomes the Arambhaka.

(ii) If a planet placed in the debilitation sign of the Pachaka becomes the Arambhaka.

(iii) The Pachaka being debilitated in the Rasi Chakra or in the Graha Chakra.

(iv) Any debilitated planet becoming the Arambhaka.

25. Varshacharya

- The Varshacharya is to be initiated from the stronger between the Bhava Lagna and its 7th sign applying the Sutra स्वामिगुरुज्ञदृग्योगोद्वितीयः. Here, as per the sequence mentioned, the priority is to be given to the aspect. Only when aspects are absent, conjunctions are to be considered.

- First, the aspect of the sign lord is to be considered. If that is absent, the aspect of Jupiter is to be considered. When that too is absent, the aspect of Mercury is to be considered. The sequence of preference in conjunctions is also to be similarly considered.
- In some cases, both the Bhava Lagna and its 7th house might not have this kind of strength. In such instances, the second kind of strength is to be applied to the Bhava Lagna Lord and the lord of its 7th sign to determine the stronger between them. Then, the Varshacharya is to be initiated from the sign of the stronger lord. Alternately, the Varshacharya can be initiated from the Bhava Lagna itself.
- For each of the Bhava Lagna Karaka Dasas, consider the way the Dasa years are calculated in the zodiacal or reverse order from the Arambhaka to the Pachaka. Then, starting from the stronger sign between Bhava Lagna and its 7th, take the Varshacharya by considering one sign per year in the same zodiacal or reverse order. Interpret the results of Varshacharya by keeping the Pachaka in the respective sign in the year and considering his exaltation, debilitation, benefic and malefic nature of planets in the signs etc.
- Another way of interpreting the Varshacharya is by blending the planetary positions in the Rasi Chakra and Graha Chakra for a particular sign ruling over particular year.

26. Upajeevya Raja Yogas

- The term *Upajeevya* refers to the position of the Raja/Atma Karakas and Amatya Karakas in the same sign or ahead or behind from each other in different Chakras without having any gaps in between.
- In these Upajeevya Raja Yogas the four Karakas – Atma Karaka, Amatya Karaka, Lagna lord and the 7th lord – are considered.
- The position of these four Karakas in the 5th and 9th signs from the Janma Lagna in the four Chakras – Rasi, Svamsa, Pada and Upapada Chakras – is considered.
- Here, using the relative positions of the Atma and Amatya Karakas in the Svamsa, Pada, Upapada and Rasi Chakras with

reference to the 5th and 9th house from the Janma Lagna, Raja Yogas and Raja Samana Yogas are proposed.

- If the Upajeevya Yogas are formed by the placement of both the Karakas in the 5th or 9th house, they result in Raja Yogas.
- Among these Yogas, when three or more Yogas are formed, the native will become a *Simhasanadhipati* (ruler of an empire or kingdom). If two Yogas are formed, the native will be a *Mandaladhipati* (ruler of a smaller kingdom). When only a single Yoga is formed, the native will be a *Kshudra Prabhu* (ruler of a very small region).
- If the Upajeevya Yoga is formed by one of the Karakas placed in the 5th or 9th house in a Chakra while the other Karaka occupies the immediately adjacent sign in another Chakra, the native will become an equal to a king in position by becoming wealthy and influential but he does not enjoy ruling power.

జైమినీ సూత్రాణి

లక్ష్మణ కృత సంస్కృత వ్యాఖ్య
(ఉ) సంపూర్ణం॥
(ప్ర)థమతః [illegible]
[illegible]

जैमिनि सूत्राणि
लक्ष्मणासूरि व्याख्या
चत्वारिंशात् सूत्रमात्रम्

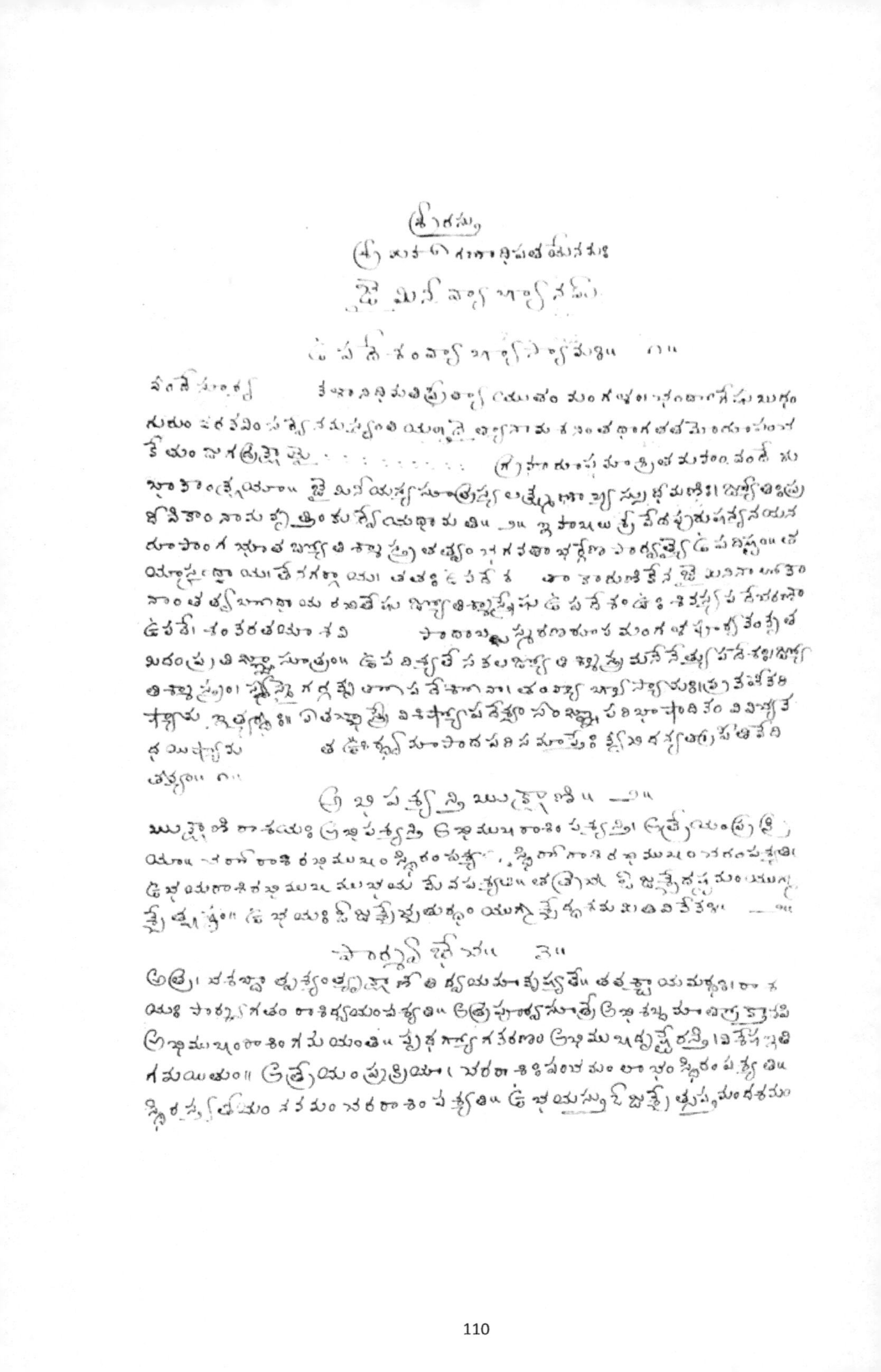

శ్రీరస్తు

[illegible]

జైమినీ [illegible]

ఉపదేశం వ్యాఖ్యాస్యామః ॥ 1 ॥

[illegible]

అభిపశ్యన్తి ఋక్షాణి ॥ 2 ॥

[illegible]

పార్శ్వభే చ ॥ 3 ॥

[illegible]

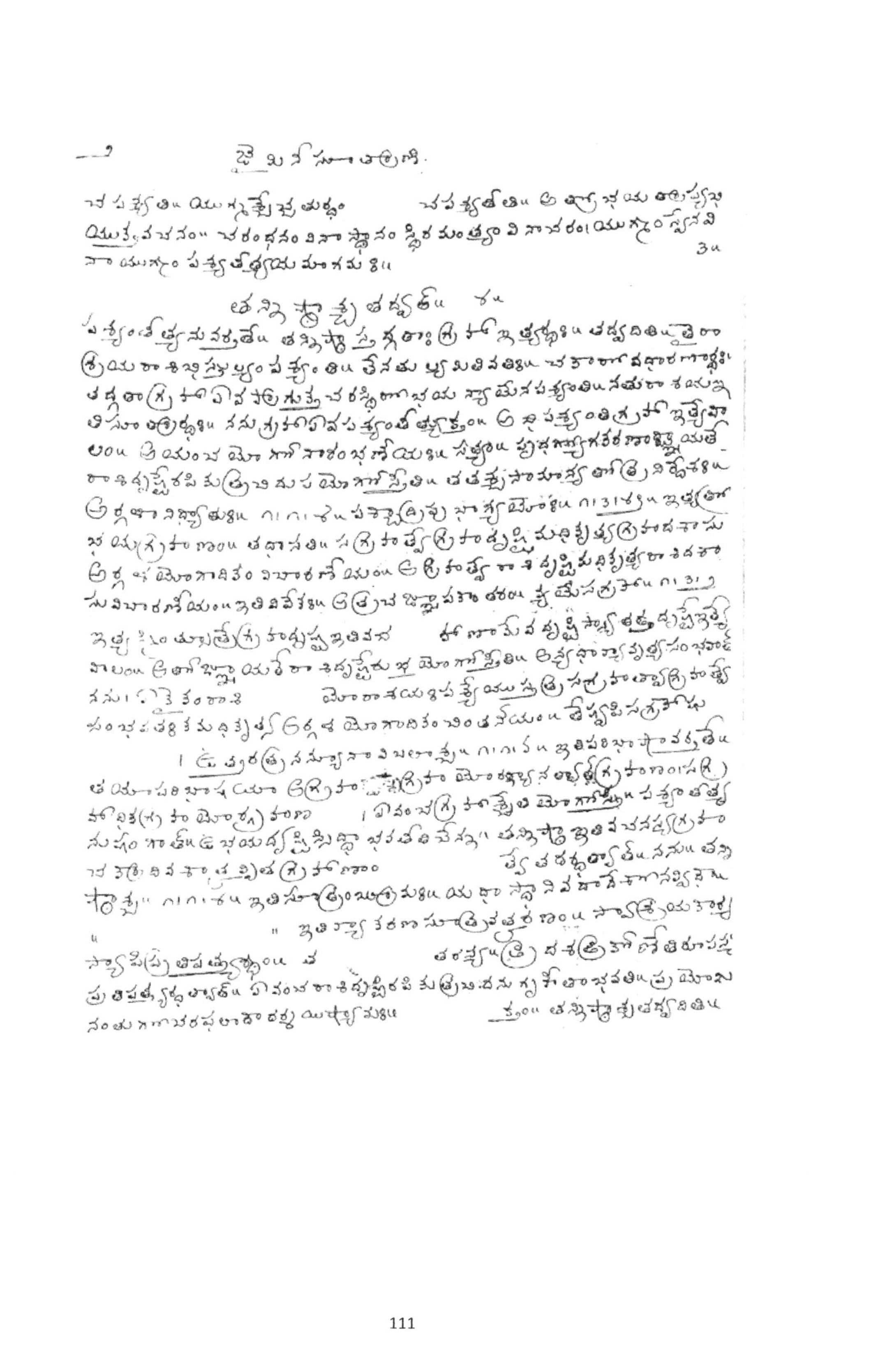

జైమిని సూత్రాణి

[illegible]

తస్మిన్ స్థానే తద్వత్ ॥ ౪॥

[illegible]

ఏవం చ శుభత్వ, పాపత్వ, యోగత్వ, నిర్బాల్యాదికం గ్రహాణాం దారాణామిత్యం

దారభాగ్యకాల స్థానగ్రహాణాం దిక్కాలేయుః ॥ ౧ ॥

యది తత్ సామాన్యోక్తేః ॥ దృష్ట గ్రహస్య ... దారభాగ్యకా

ల స్థాన గ్రహా భవన్తి ... [illegible]

[illegible]

[illegible]

[illegible]

[illegible]

[illegible] ॥ ౧౩౨ ॥ [illegible]

[illegible] ॥ ౧౩౩ ॥

[illegible] ॥ ౨ ॥

కామస్థానం భాగ్యకాలం ... ॥ ౩ ॥

[illegible]

[illegible]

[illegible] ॥ ౩ ॥

[illegible] ॥ ౪ ॥

[illegible]

[illegible]

[illegible]

[illegible]

[illegible]

[illegible] ॥ ౫ ॥

దారభాగ్యకాల [illegible]

[illegible]

[illegible]

[illegible] ॥ ౧౩౪ ॥ [illegible]

[illegible] ॥ ౫ ॥

[illegible] ॥ ౬ ॥

[illegible]

జైమినీ సూత్రాణి

తి భాగ్య లాభ [illegible] ఇతి [illegible] భాగ్య [illegible] [illegible] మకరస్య [illegible]
రాజ యోగః సింహం ద్రష్టవ్య భాగ్య యోగ ఇతి రాజయోగ [illegible] భాగ్య [illegible] సిద్ధం [illegible]
[illegible] ఫలకే లాభ [illegible] [illegible] తథాహి కన్యాది [illegible]
మకరాంతి [illegible] [illegible] [illegible] [illegible]
[illegible] భాగ్య యోగః [illegible]
పరి [illegible] దశా పంచ వర్షా [illegible] మకరాది [illegible]
[illegible] లాభ [illegible] [illegible]

ఉదాహరణం

శకాబ్దాః ౧౫౪౮ [illegible] సంవత్సర ఫాల్గున మాసం [illegible] [illegible] [illegible]
ఘటికాః ౬॥ [illegible] జననం॥

లగ్నం ౧౧।౬।౨౦।	గురుః ౧।।।
తత్ర స్ఫుట గ్రహాః॥	శుక్రః ౧౦।౨౩।౨౦
రవిః ౧౧।౨౭।౫౩	శనిః ౨।౧౦।౩౮
చంద్రః ౨।౭౫।౫౭	రాహుః ౨౧।౨౭।౪౮
కుజః ౨౧।౧౧।౩౨	[illegible] లగ్నం [illegible] [illegible]
బుధః ౦।౧౬।౧౦	

[illegible] [illegible] [illegible] ౧।[illegible]
[illegible] ఘటికా [illegible] దశ పంచ [illegible] లాభ
[illegible] [illegible] [illegible]
[illegible] ఘటికా [illegible] ౧।౩।౨౮। ఇతి [illegible]
[illegible] [illegible]
[illegible] లగ్న ఘటికా [illegible] [illegible]
[illegible] [illegible]
[illegible] [illegible] [illegible] [illegible] యోగ
[illegible] [illegible] యోగ [illegible]
[illegible] రాజ యోగ [illegible] [illegible]
[illegible] [illegible] [illegible]
తథాహి॥
మకరాది దశా [illegible]
[illegible] దశా [illegible] [illegible]
[illegible] దశా [illegible] ౩ [illegible] [illegible]

౭)　　　　జైమిని సూత్రాణి

ఓం(త) బుధ యోగాత్ (బు) ఓల్కాష్ఠ ఆకాశ్య వశముద్భ్యం శతిష్ఠ — ౨౮॥ వత్కపరంప్ర ప్రాస్య దశా దశశల్లా। తత్ర భాగ్య కారక త్రిగ్రహం ద్వాయుసంబంధా దత్వ్య ప్రయుక్త తతః మిథునదశా శతల్ల ౩॥ తతః కర్కట దశా ద్యాదశ వల్లా॥ ౭॥ తత్ర త్రిషు మబుధ వక్త్రరాశి ౩॥ కర్కట కారక పతేర్న్యం(త్రి)స్య మిథునగత త్వేన తస్య మూంది ఖండ కేల్వన చరాం తత్త్రిపు త్రి యోగాం దృష్ట్య త్వం॥ బుధ దృష్టేః రాహు యోగ త్రివదత్వం చేతి మహోనార్నతి కాలః॥

వతాష్య ఆంశ ద్వల్లాణిః తతో మీనఖండ త్రిపక్షః॥ త్రి మారకయో గాద్యాగ్న్య మారకయోగాత్తే తత్ కాలః॥

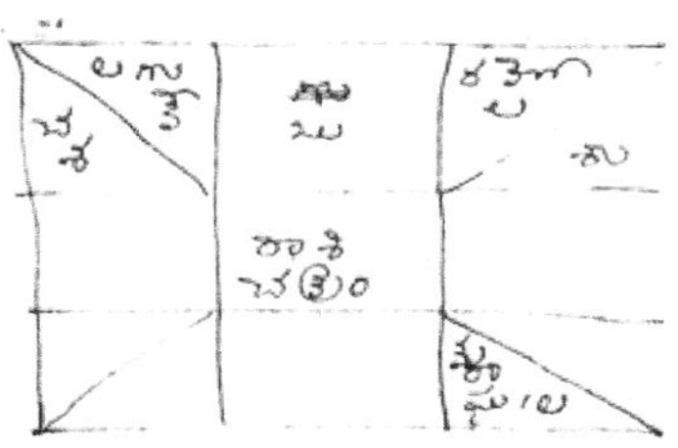

ఉదాహరణాంతరం.

శ్రీ తతః పరముదాహరణాం। శకాబ్దాః ౧౮౧౬॥　　　　　జయం భాద్రపదం మాసః — ౨౧ తిథి ఉదయాది ఘటికాః ౨౭.౪౨
శ్రీ　యాజ్ఞవల్క్య భాష్యకార్య జననం॥

లగ్నం ౧౩।౨౧-౨　　　　　బుధః
శ్రీ(త్ర)స్తు అత్ర కాశ్య　　గురుః ౧౦।౫।—౨౭
రవిః ౫।—౨౫।　　　　　శుక్రః ౪। ౨౧।—౨౭
చంద్రః ౧—౨౫।—౨౪　　　　శనిః ౮। ౭। ౩౭
కుజః ౮।—౨౫।—౨౯।౭॥ రాహుః ౫। —౨। ౪౮
కేతుః ౧౧।—౨।౪౮। ఆయుః ౭౦॥ కాల లగ్నం॥
ఘటికాల గ్నం స్త్ర పత్రః॥

శ్రీ(త్రి) విలగ్న ద్వితీ చెప్రచేసన వనాతేః(త్రీ)ః సత్త్వ లాంఛ యోగ త్రితి ౧౧।౩।—౨౧॥ సూత్రాణ్యాపి వి శేష రాజ యోగాః। తద్యథా। లగ్నం గురుః పశ్యతి। సప్తమ శాతి లగ్న సప్త మకా లాంశ్యం(ద)ః పశ్యతి॥ తథా గురు శుక్రయో ద్వయ్య స్యాన్యద్రా తయో రగ్గ ఆ విషయత్వం॥ తదాది కర్మ స్థం త్రైస్వ వయోగద　　　యత్వం॥ ద్విత్రీ కారక యోగ్యాం బాంధవ్య తత్ర యుత్వతి యయో గ్రహ బాహ్య యోగ సహ కాలత్వం యోగాంతర కర్త్వ ల్లాంచ। యుక్త్యపి। చంద్ర।　　　　యుక్తత్వా।

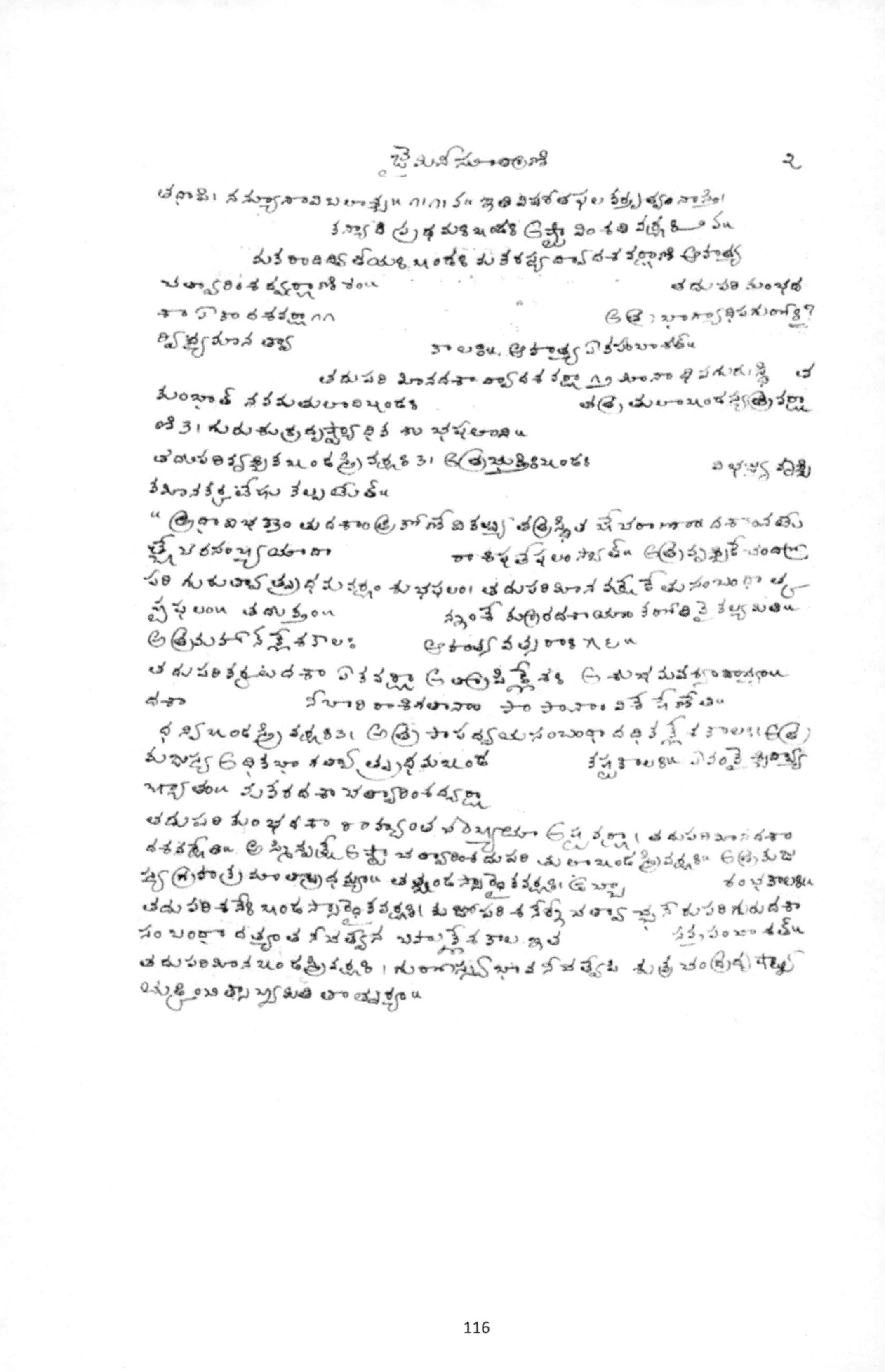

[illegible]

[illegible]

సశుభే దృష్టే బంధ మోక్షయోః ॥ ౧౨ ॥

[illegible]

[illegible]

[illegible] ||౧౩||

తస్య భ్రాతా ||౧౪||

[illegible]

తస్య మాతా ||౧౫|| తస్య పుత్రః ||౧౬||

ఇతి సూత్రద్వయేన ప్రసిద్ధమేవ [illegible] ||౧౫|౧౬||

తస్య జ్ఞాతిః ||౧౭||

[illegible] తదనంతరం పుత్ర [illegible] జ్ఞాతికారకత్వం ||౧౭||

తస్య దారాశ్చ ||౧౮||

[illegible] ||౧౮||

మాతృసహ పుత్రమేకే సమామనంతి ||౧౯||

[illegible] ||౧౯||

భగిన్యస్తథా శ్యాలః కనీయాన్ జననీ చేతి ||౨౦||

[illegible]

[illegible]

[illegible]

౧౬) జైమినీసూత్రాణి

[illegible]

ఉదాహరణం.

[illegible]

[illegible]

రవిః ౧।౨౩।౧౫। శనిః ।౨।౬।౪౪
చంద్రః ౫।౬।౧౪॥ రాహుః ౭।౧౬।౪౪
కుజః ౩।౧౬।౩ కేతుః ౩।౧౬।౪౪
బుధః ౧। । । లగ్నం మీనం
గురుః ౬।౪।౩౧॥ భావలగ్నం వృషభః
శుక్రః ౧।౧౩।౯౪॥ [illegible]

శ్రీ [illegible]

[illegible]

[illegible]

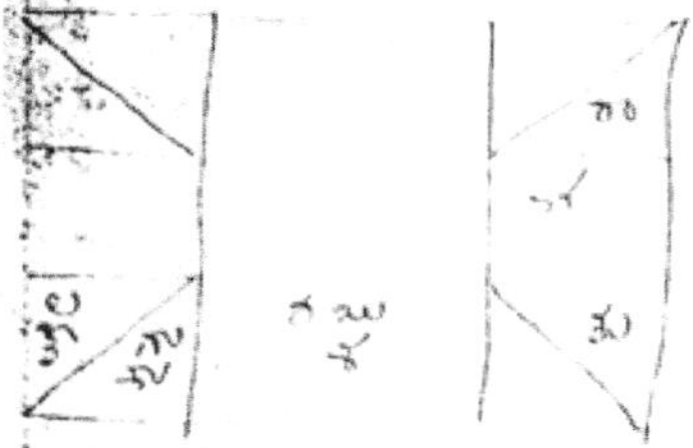

[illegible]

లగ్నం [illegible]	గురుకి [illegible]
రవికి [illegible]	శుక్రుకి [illegible]
చంద్రుకి [illegible]	శనికి [illegible]
కుజుకి [illegible]	రాహువు
బుధుకి [illegible]	కేతువు

[illegible]

౧౮. జైమినీ సూత్రాణి

ఉదాహరణం

కే		కు
	రాశి	చ బు
ల		శుక్ర

శకాబ్దాః ౧౭౧౩ ఖర సంవత్సర వైశాఖమాస
శుద్ధ తదియ ఉదయాది ఘటికాః ౩౨।౧౦
... సావిత్రీశ్చ జననం॥

స్ఫుటగ్రహాః.

రవిః
చంద్రః ౮।౧౮।౭।౧। కుజః ౧౧।౧౧।౧౩।౪౦ బుధః
౮।౧౪।౩౫ గురుః ౭।౪।౭।౪।౧౨। శుక్రః ౫।౭।౪౮ శనిః ౭।౧।౧౧
రాహుః ౭।౧౨।౭౬। కేతుః ౫।౧౨।౭౬। లగ్నం ౫।౬।౩౨॥

అధిక భాగ కలస్య గురోః ... [illegible] ... సమాప్తి
గురు ... [illegible]
... [illegible]
... [illegible]
... [illegible]
... [illegible]
... [illegible]

ఉదాహరణం॥

... [illegible]

	ల	
	రాశి	
కు	బు	

శకాబ్దాః ౧౭౪౦ ... సంవత్సర ...
... ౧౩ తిథి ఉదయాది ఘటికాః
౭౭।౧౦ ... జననం॥

స్ఫుటగ్రహాః

లగ్నం ౦।౭।౧౦ రవిః ౭।౧౬।౭।౧। ...॥
... ౪।౧౪।౬ బుధః ౬।౧౦।౧౩

గురుః ౧౦।౧౦।౧౩ శుక్రః ॥ శనిః॥ ॥

రాహుః॥ ॥ కేతుః॥

అధిక భాగ ... [illegible]
... [illegible]

... [illegible]
... [illegible]
... [illegible]

From the Author

Raghava Bhatta's

JATAKA SARA SANGRAHA

Publisher: Self, Pages: 643

Jaimini system is a highly practical method which helps its practitioners to reach quick conclusions regarding the events and their timing in the life of a native. The rules are simple and straight forward and the Dasa durations can be calculated easily in mind.

Jataka Sara Sangraha is a unique work in this branch of Jyotisha where the author ingeniously presents his material in a logical fashion drawing from the Jaimini Sutras and Vruddha Karikas. For the first time in the literature of Jaimini astrology the author explains the application of all the Ayurdasas by giving a single example Horoscope. This is one of the rare works where numerous Ayurdasas and Phalita Dasas are explained in detail.

The treatise is divided into three Parichchedas or chapters. The first chapter deals with the methods of longevity determination of a native and explains the Ayurdasas which help to predict the time of death of the native and his relatives like parents, siblings, spouse and so on. The second chapter deals with different Phalita Dasas which help to predict the timing of various events in a native's life. The final and third chapter explains many Yogas. For the convenience of presentation and to maintain continuity, I have segregated the contents of the first chapter under four titles: Ayurdaya Determination, Ayurdasas for the native, Ayurdasas for the native's relatives, and Nature and place of death of the native and his relatives.

Jataka Sara Sangraha is a must to grasp the nuances of Jaimini System and gain mastery over the subject.

SARFAROSH

A Naadi exposition of the lives of Indian Revolutionaries

Publisher: Notion Press, Pages: 516

The life events of 108 revolutionaries belonging to the Indian Independence Struggle have been explained in a novel way using the Nandi Naadi principles discovered by the author.

Besides the astrological angle, this book presents the biographical details of the revolutionaries, their poignant tales of courage and struggle against a giant colonial power and the tremendous sacrifices they made for the cause of mother India.

This book is indispensable for anyone who wants to grasp the application of Nandi Naadi principles to various facets of human life including longevity, mode of death, illness, misfortunes, married life, progeny, career and so on.

BLIND CHART ANALYSIS

Predicting past and background of unknown people

Publisher: Self, Pages: 448

'Blind Chart Analysis' is a procedure in which an astrologer predicts the past events and present condition of a native only by looking into the horoscope, without having a prior knowledge about the native. Astrologers practice this method for many reasons: for birth-time rectification, to bring faith in the client about the efficacy of astrology, to test the astrological techniques, to find out which method suits best for the given case, and to demonstrate his/her predictive abilities. To do blind chart analysis successfully an astrologer should have very sound knowledge of the subject, vast experience, good intuition and a bit of luck also.

This book presents 100 cases of Blind Chart Analysis of people who approached the author for astrological consultation. This is a book, first of its kind, where the author demonstrates the method of Blind Chart Analysis by explaining the astrological reasons for the queries he asked the natives and for the responses he got. This work impresses the reader about the power and utility of Jyotisha in general and Nandi Naadi methods in particular. A must for anyone who wishes to gain command over the art of prediction

RASI TULYA VATSARA DASA

A simple and unique method of timing events

Publisher: Self, Pages: 174

Imagine a dasa system which can broadly indicate the events that can occur in a year in the life of a native? How would it be if we could arrive at the particular year of a Vimshottari Antara for an event to manifest which can then be zeroed in with the aid of transits? The **'Rasi-tulya-vatsara dasa'** is precisely such a system.

This book explains the general rules and specific rules of RTVD system discovered by the author and demonstrates its applicability to various branches of human life with the help of more than 150 practical illustrations.

The topics covered in the book include:
Longevity and Death: Balarishta, Alpayu, Madhyayu and Deerghayu; **Marital Issues**: Happy and Stable Marriages, Delayed Marriages, Elopement and Love marriages, Divorce and Separation cases, Multiple Marriages, Widowhood and Loss of Spouse, Death along with spouse, Killing own spouse, Killed by Spouse; **Progeny**: Child birth, Delayed child birth, Miscarriages, infantile deaths and assisted pregnancy, Death of Mother at the time of Delivery, Death along with children, Death and misfortune to children, Killing own children, Killed by own son; **Parents:** Death of Parents, Accidents, diseases, and misfortunes to Parents, RajaYogas to the parents; **Siblings**: Birth of Siblings, Happy events to Siblings, Death of Siblings, Killing own sibling, Killed by own sibling, Misfortunes to the Siblings; **Mishaps:** Diseases, Accidents, and Assaults and other mishaps; **Wealth and Finance:** Financial Gains, Lotteries, Gamblings etc, Loss of Money, financial bankruptcy, Purchase of immovable properties and vehicles, Loss of property; **Profession, Fame, Awards, and Disgrace:** Beginning of career, Promotions in Jobs, Problems at workplace, suspensions, loss of job, insults, Political careers, Crimes and Arrests, Awards, achievements, and fame.

This book is very helpful not only to master the simple yet effective system of RTVD but also to gain insights in judging the horoscope to assess the potential promise for an event.

APPLIED VEDIC ASTROLOGY

Compilation of Published Articles

Publisher: Self, Pages: 290

This book contains eighteen articles of the author published in various astrological journals, starting from 2003 to 2017. Contents of the book include: *I. The Bhagavad Gita-The Astrologer's Guide, II. Sun's Role in Judging Profession, III. Guru Chandala Yoga and Religiousness, IV. Eighth House and Astrologers, V. Poets, Musicians and Venus, VI. Ninth House and Unconventional Marriages, VII. A Critical Analysis of Asura and Sarala Yogas, VIII. Astrology in Ayurvedic classics, IX. Astrology and Homosexuality, X. Integrating Multiple Predictive Tools - A Case Study, XI. Astrology and Paedophiles, XII. Health Issues of Relatives - Astrological Clues, XIII. Jatakabhanga or Failure-in-Life Yogas, XIV.*

Mars and Earth Science Professions, XV. Astrological Study of Rape Cases, XVI. How Transits Affect Dasa-Bhukti Lords, XVII. Decoding Devakeralam, and XVIII. Mahamahopadhyaya Sri Madhura Krishnamurthy Sastry - An Astrological Portrait.

eBook editions of all the books are available at Amazon. Paperback editions are also available across USA, Europe and Japan through the Amazon platform. For paperback copies in India, write to:

raj91979@gmail.com
rajesh_kotekal@rediffmail.com

Made in the USA
Las Vegas, NV
30 October 2023

79977901R00079